Not Worth the Paper..?

THE EFFECTIVENESS OF LEGAL PROTECTION FOR WOMEN & CHILDREN EXPERIENCING DOMESTIC VIOLENCE

Jackie Barron

Published by the Women's Aid Federation England Ltd.
© WAFE Ltd. 1990
ISBN: 0 907817 40 8

Copies available from:
WAFE Ltd.
PO Box 391
Bristol BS99 7WS
Price: £6.50

Typeset & Printed by
Sheffield Women's Printing Co-op (TU) Ltd. (0742) 753180

CONTENTS

PREFACE:
WHO WE ARE

A number of women have been involved in producing this report and in the research which provided the basis for it. In writing this account, we have therefore mostly used the collective pronoun "we" to signify this joint responsibility, except where it seemed necessary to do otherwise. "We" are all women who share the aims and ideals of Women's Aid Federation (England) (WAFE), and most of us are or have been active members of local Women's Aid groups affiliated to WAFE.

The study which is described here was undertaken by Jackie Barron, Anjali Gupta and Parveen Alam. They were accountable to the Research Advisory Group (appointed by WAFE) which provided guidance throughout. The members of the Research Advisory Group (not all of whom were able to participate throughout) are listed below, with a brief resume of their relevant experience. The money for the study and this publication was provided by the Department of Health and WAFE.

Jackie, as the only full-time researcher who has been present throughout, has been responsible for the major part of the writing of this report. Anjali wrote the basis for Chapter 5, and Parveen contributed ideas to this chapter. All chapters have been read in draft form, and amended, by the Research Advisory Group, and by certain members of the National Co-ordinating Group (NCG) of WAFE, who volunteered themselves. As far as possible, we have tried to reflect the views of all those women who have taken the trouble to read and comment on various drafts, but the final responsibility must rest with Jackie, and with those members of the Research Advisory Group who were able to be present in the final stages before publication.

Members of the WAFE Research Advisory Group

Lema Daley: Housing Worker, National Office, 1988-89.

Christina Ghaitey: Christina has a Diploma in Social Leadership from St.Francis Xavier University, Canada. Recently, she has been working in community development, and is currently Outreach Worker for Clapham Women's Aid. She is a member of the Domestic Violence Network in Lambeth.

Gill Hague: Gill has worked as both a paid worker and a volunteer in Bristol Women's Aid and is currently Chair. She has also been active in Women's Aid Federation for a number of years. She is a trained social worker who has held a variety of positions as residential social worker, officer in the voluntary housing sector and lecturer in social work and social policy.

Nicola Harwin: Nicola currently works as National Co-ordinator of WAFE, based at the national office in Bristol. She has been involved in Women's Aid since 1976, as a volunteer, refuge worker, management committee member and voluntary Regional Co-ordinator. She has been active in the women's movement since 1970, and is a trained community worker.

Marjorie Homer: Has a B.Sc. (Hons.) in Social Sciences, and is co-author of *Private Violence: Public Shame* (CRAWC, 1984). She has been involved in Middlesbrough refuge for 11 years, as volunteer, Management Committee member, Researcher (1981-3) and refuge worker (1985 to present). She has also been a member of the North East Legal Action Research Group, and has been involved in inter-agency initiatives, including a police initiated Working Party on police response to domestic violence in Cleveland.

Pam Jobbins: Pam has been employed by Durham Women's Aid since 1982. She has also been involved in various sub-groups of NWAF/WAFE, including the Pamphlets Group, the Finance Group and the National Co-ordinating Group. She was a member of the group which compiled the WAFE booklet, "You can't beat a woman". She has also been a member of the joint research project formed from the North East region of WAFE and the North East Legal Action Group Women's Section. This project looked into the efficacy of injunctions and protection orders, and since September 1989, Pam has been writing up the results, which will be published shortly.

Hilary Koe: Lecturer in Law at the University of East Anglia. Hilary has been a member of Peterborough Women's Aid for several years, both as a worker and on the support group. She has also been co-opted onto Scunthorpe Women's Aid in an advisory capacity. She is writing up her research on the effectiveness of legal protection when there is violence between partners, for an Ll.M. at UEA, and is hoping to do some research on the police in the near future.

Hilary Land: Professor of Social Policy at Royal Holloway and Bedford New College, University of London. Hilary was part of the "Why be a wife?" campaign in the 1970s. Her concern, both as an academic and an activist is with the financial and legal relationship between men and women in the family, and the ways in which the state, through the taxation and social security systems, reinforces women's dependence on men.

Ellen Malos: Ellen is a Research Fellow in the Department of Social

Policy and Social Planning at the University of Bristol, where she has been involved in teaching and in policy-related research in a number of areas, most recently in the field of child-care legislation. In 1990, she will be carrying out a three month review of policy, practice and research on the use of bed and breakfast hotels for the homeless. She is a founder member of Bristol Women's Aid and has worked as both a volunteer and paid refuge worker. She has been active in the Women's Movement since 1969.

Ann Smith: Support Group member, Manchester Women's Aid 2, since 1987. Ann is currently employed as a researcher by Birmingham Social Services.

The Researchers

Parveen Alam: Has worked for several years as a voluntary worker in Bristol, and within Asian communities. She has had personal experience of the problems of marital breakdown.

Jackie Barron: Has a B.A. from Hatfield Polytechnic and a Ph.D. from University College of Wales, Cardiff. Previous research has included studies of women in local politics, and she was responsible for writing up the research undertaken by the NWAF Legal Sub-Group on the Domestic Violence Act. (NWAF, 1980). Jackie has been a member of Bristol Women's Aid for several years, and is also a volunteer on the WAFE national Helpline.

Anjali Gupta: Has a B.A. in Social Science from Bristol Polytechnic, and has worked until very recently for Kingswood Women's Aid.

About the Report

We have tried to write this report in such a way that it is accessible to anyone who is interested in the issues involved. Inevitably, some sections contain complex technical information which it is difficult to set out in a simple or straightforward way. This may be particularly the case with Chapter 2, on the law. We have tried to write each chapter so that it is self-contained, and readers who are less interested in these technical matters may therefore proceed to later chapters without feeling that they have missed any of the substance of the research itself. (This inevitably means that there is a certain amount of repetition of key points in several chapters of the report.)

There is a Glossary of technical terms at the end of the book.

We have included many direct quotations from our interviews in order to illustrate the kinds of material on which we are basing our conclusions. All our interviewees have been given numbers and sometimes details have been changed to preserve confidentiality. (For example, whenever a proper name is included in any of the quotes, this will be a pseudonym.)

Acknowledgements

We would like to thank the Department of Health for providing most of the funding which made this research possible; Bristol Polytechnic for administering the payment of Jackie's salary, and providing facilities for her and Anjali; Pat Gubbins, finance worker at WAFE national office, for administering the rest of the finances associated with this study; Caroline McKinlay, WAFE national worker, for arranging for the publication of this report; the Lord Chancellor's Department, and many individual judges, for allowing one of us to observe county court injunction cases held in chambers; the Magistrates' Courts' Committees in Avon and Kendal for agreeing that we could sit in on personal protection applications in the respective magistrates' courts; the women who were prepared to talk to us about their experiences; all the women who have read and commented on this report prior to publication; and the various legal personnel, refuge workers, advice workers and others whom we interviewed, but cannot name. One court clerk was particularly helpful in putting us in touch with other individuals whose experiences were relevant, and we are very grateful for his efforts.

CHAPTER 1:
INTRODUCTION

The study we report on here was designed as a small-scale one year investigation into the use and effectiveness of the legal protection available to women and children threatened by domestic violence. Our main emphasis, as members of Women's Aid, is on the women's perspectives and we have evaluated the adequacy and shortcomings of the remedies and services provided in terms of this perspective throughout.

The Nature and Extent of Domestic Violence

In this report, we are defining "domestic violence" as physical or mental cruelty, threats, or abuse, which women experience from their male partners, who, in most cases, are living with them[1]. We will use the terms "husband" and "partner" interchangeably, whether or not the couple are legally married, except where their marital status is significant to the outcome of the case. In some cases, the children living with the couple are also experiencing abuse, but this is not a central focus of the current study, though we are of course concerned that the available legislation also protects the children of the family effectively.

Domestic violence is not a new phenomenon, nor is it exclusive to western capitalist societies like our own. In many — perhaps most — cultures, male violence towards wives, girlfriends and daughters has been widespread, and appears to have been tacitly accepted and condoned both by the community and the law. The ideology of male dominance and authority is, today, still upheld by legal, political and economic institutions: for example — and in spite of recent cosmetic changes in social security and taxation — the nuclear family is still regarded as an economic unit with a male "head" on whom the woman and children are financially and socially dependent; and the growing number of one parent families seems to have done little to change popular beliefs (endorsed by politicians and the media) that the nuclear family, with clearly defined gender roles, is still the ideal norm.

Concern about this situation is also far from new. Early campaigners for women's rights regarded the issue as an important one, and there were several attempts in Britain during the nineteenth century to ameliorate the position of abused women. Reformers such as Frances Power Cobbe, John Stuart Mill, Elizabeth Cady Stanton and Mary Wollstonecraft all challenged women's subordination, and their efforts helped to pave the way for legal reforms from the mid-nineteenth century onwards. (Chapter 2 outlines the current law).

The exact extent of male domestic violence is unknown, though there is

1

no doubt that it is extremely widespread. One study, for example (Dobash and Dobash, 1980) found that 25% of *reported* violent crime was wife assault, and we know that a high proportion of such assaults are never reported to the police (or anyone else), or, if reported, are "no-crimed" so that they never appear in any published statistics (Coleman and Bottomley, 1976; Pahl, 1982; Hanmer *et al.*, 1989; Edwards, 1989). Other studies have estimated that more than one in a hundred marriages may be characterised by severe and repeated physical violence (Marsden and Owens, 1975; Marsden, 1978), and that, at some point, as many as one in three relationships may be violent (Borkowski *et al.*, 1983.) The nature of domestic violence is such that women, out of a mistaken sense of shame, will try to keep it secret for as long as possible, so that there is considerable under-reporting, and none of the available figures can be accepted as accurate with any confidence (Smith, 1989). Nevertheless, all the evidence that we have suggests that male violence is a "normal" rather than exceptional behaviour, and that it is aimed at reinforcing men's authority within their relationships and their homes.

Summary of Previous Research

There have been a number of studies of women's experiences of domestic violence, based primarily on interviews with women in refuges (see particularly Dobash and Dobash, 1980; Pahl, 1985; Homer *et al.*, 1984). Several books and articles on related topics have also appeared recently (Yllo and Bograd, 1988; Hanmer *et al.*, 1989; Edwards, 1989; Kelly, 1989). None of these has, however, looked directly at the issues with which we are concerned here. Among British studies, the two most relevant are those by Lorraine Radford (1989), and Kathryn McCann (1983, 1985) who have looked at aspects of the law relating to domestic violence (see below) [2].

In the absence of comparable previous studies, we see our research as, in part, a feasibility study aimed at exploring the relevant issues and the various ways in which they could most successfully be approached. In some respects, it follows an earlier unfunded study undertaken by volunteers from National Women's Aid Federation (as it then was) in 1978 (see NWAF, 1980). It is disheartening that, more than ten years later, we are finding many of the same results; for example, the reluctance of courts to grant exclusion orders, or to add powers of arrest to an injunction, inconsistency between judges, and problems in enforcement.

Kathy McCann's study focused on the use of the magistrates' courts and was based on her examination of court records and interviews with twenty-eight women who had used the legal procedure. She also (with Pat Brown and Sarah Blandy, under the auspices of Sheffield Women's Aid) monitored the workings of the Domestic Proceedings and Magistrates' Courts' Act, 1978, for a short period in several areas. She concluded that both the police and the courts tend to treat domestic

2

assaults as a social rather than a criminal or legal problem, and are, in many cases, reluctant to intervene; the effectiveness of the law is therefore, in practice, limited by sexist attitudes, and pre — existing gender inequalities throughout society.

Lorraine Radford examined case records, talked to solicitors and interviewed twenty women who had complained of their partners' behaviour (mostly violence) in their divorce petitions. She found that many women had experienced incompetent or slow solicitors, or had difficulties in finding a solicitor who would take on the case at all. She concluded that solicitors' "professional" judgements (for example, that there was no point in applying for an order since the court would not grant it) took precedence over the woman's need for protection. She also detected a marked inconsistency between different judges and different courts.

In addition to empirical investigations, there have been a number of articles, mainly by lawyers, commenting on particular aspects of or difficulties with the existing law. Among the most recent of these, we would like to make particular mention of the articles by Roger Hamilton (1984), Rae and Levin (1983) and Patrick Parkinson (1986) on the relevance, for married women, of the Domestic Violence and Matrimonial Proceedings Act 1986 (as opposed to the Matrimonial Homes Act, 1983); Sarah Maidment's articles on the effectiveness of the civil law (1985) and the relevance of criminal prosecution of violent men (1983)[3]; and Catherine Williams' article (1988) on the links between matrimonial law and long-term housing for women made homeless by domestic violence. The existing legal provision is clearly set out in the Law Commission's recent Working Paper, "Domestic Violence and the Occupation of the Matrimonial Home" (W.P.113, HMSO, 1989), and other relevant literature is included in the bibliography. (See also Chapter 2).

There have also been a number of more general studies on women and the law (see for example, Atkins and Hoggatt, 1984; Brophy and Smart, 1985; Edwards, 1985b; and Smart, 1984, 1989). Most of these studies tend to endorse the view that our legal system operates according to certain systematic biases which reflect our male dominated society and culture. In particular, the law continues to support a family structure in which male and female roles are clearly delineated, and in which, as a consequence, women's dependency is a fundamental feature. Some have gone on to argue that part of the power of legal knowledge (or legal "discourse") is that it disqualifies other forms of knowledge — including, particularly, feminism — which are incompatible with it. (See Smart, 1989) For example, in a rape trial, the legal view that certain kinds of evidence, such as the woman's sexual history, are "relevant" to the case not only takes precedence over, but actually rules out, the feminist argument that past events have no bearing on the issue of consent on this occasion. While there are clearly immense problems here, we still feel that there is a place for constructive criticism and piecemeal reform of the law and its implementation, as pragmatic measures which may help some women in the short term. Similarly, we believe that studies like our own can help to highlight persisting problems which must be addressed whenever new legislation or changes to existing law are proposed.

The Research Design: A Summary

The funding for this study came initially from the Department of Health, which provided a lump sum grant for the purpose of research to the Women's Aid Federation (England). As researchers, we are directly accountable to WAFE (specifically through the Research Advisory Group set up for this purpose), and the Department of Health therefore bears no responsibility either for the research design and methodology or for the findings and recommendations which follow from them. WAFE specified the original guidelines within which we carried out the research. On the basis of these guidelines, one of us (Jackie) then put forward a research proposal which was accepted by WAFE, and thereafter modified and developed as a result of practical considerations and with the agreement of the WAFE Research Group.

We all believed that it was important for there to be considerable input from black women, so that their needs would not be marginalised, and that issues of particular importance to them could be adequately explored. Jackie initially hoped to put forward a joint proposal with a black woman or women who was interested in working in this area. Unfortunately, because of tight time constraints, she was unable to make contact with an appropriate woman with whom to develop a joint proposal. Her second hope was that if a black woman put in an independent proposal, the money could be shared and the women could work to a considerable extent together, on linked projects. No black woman put in a proposal, however. In the absence of these options, we therefore agreed that a black co-researcher should be appointed as soon as possible, and also that black women should be invited and encouraged to join the Research Advisory Group. The problems we encountered will be discussed below.

The original proposal included the following features:
1. observation in county and magistrates' courts, when applications for matrimonial injunctions and personal protection orders were being heard.
2. interviews with a small number of women (c.45) who had experienced domestic violence recently and who may or may not have tried to gain protection from their violent partner through the legal system.
3. Follow up interviews, where appropriate, to explore the continuing effectiveness of the remedy chosen.
4. interviews with a small number of professionals (e.g. solicitors, social workers, probation officers) who in their work might be called upon to advise or support women and children experiencing violence within

4

the home.

5. an examination of the statistics provided by the Lord Chancellor's Office and the Home Office regarding use of the courts for these purposes.

Our approach was primarily a qualitative one, as this was most appropriate to the exploratory nature of the study and accorded best with our feminist perspective.(See Oakley, 1981; Finch, 1983; Graham, 1983).

One central focus of these enquiries would be the use (and non-use) of injunctions or personal protection orders. We were particularly interested in the appropriateness and effectiveness of these remedies, for women in certain kinds of situations. Our personal experience, and that of other women in Women's Aid, was that court orders were only of limited use, in that only rarely — if at all — did they seem to prevent further violence or harassment to women seeking protection for themselves and their children. However, we recognised that women who enter refuges or who seek advice from the WAFE Helpline or from local advice centres may perhaps over-represent those who have experienced repeated problems; in other words, those women who have successfully obtained effective remedies through the courts may not need to use our services. For that reason, we believed it was important that our sample of women interviewees was not drawn primarily from refuges but should try to represent the variety of experiences, including women who felt no need of the protection or support which Women's Aid could offer, and those who did not know of, or chose not to get in touch with, a local or national Women's Aid organisation.

For similar reasons, we felt it was important to represent the experiences of rural as well as urban women and to base the research in at least two contrasting areas, in different parts of England. There is some evidence from nationally published figures, that courts in different parts of the country may vary in their readiness to grant injunctions and protection orders, to attach powers of arrest to such an order, or to commit a man to prison for breach of an order or undertaking. It is likely also that within each court circuit, individual judges and magistrates may differ in their attitudes and practices. Early on, we narrowed the possible research areas down to two alternatives: Birmingham combined with Devon (centring on Okehampton); or Bristol and Cumbria, with particular reference to Kendal. Neither of these rural areas had refuges nearby, and this, we felt, compounded the isolation and lack of options available to women in these areas (see Ellis, 1983). The urban areas were reasonably accessible to us (as researchers living in Bristol) and in different court circuits (with possible different practices and procedures) from the respective rural areas selected. Our final choice was Bristol and Cumbria.

Another consideration was the importance we wanted to give to the experiences of certain groups: in particular, black women, and women with disabilities. We believed that the available legal remedies might be even less appropriate for these women than for white and/or able-bodied women. For example, there could be difficulties regarding accessibility (of solicitors and courts), communication (with legal personnel and other professionals), cultural barriers, or special housing needs which could not be accommodated within the standardised legal system and procedures. Black women, who experience racism in every area of their lives, have no reason to trust white professionals, and may understandably resist consulting them, however great their needs. In addition, the immigration status of some Asian women may be dependent on their husbands, thus creating special problems for them in leaving home or claiming social security benefits. (See Alibhai, 1989.) We also felt it was important to represent the experiences of women of all ages, all marital statuses, and with or without dependent children, as any or all of these criteria might influences the choices a woman might make, or the options available to her, and might also affect the attitudes and decisions of solicitors, magistrates and other court personnel. Women with drug or alcohol related problems might also experience particular difficulties which we have unfortunately not been able to explore adequately in this study.

Implementation of Research Design: Initial Problems

The research funding commenced in October 1988, when one researcher (Jackie) was in post. At this stage, there were two immediate tasks:
1. To gain access to observe court proceedings — which, in cases of this kind, are normally held in chambers, i.e. with the public excluded.
2. To appoint a co-researcher who should be a black woman, in order to a) facilitate contact with other black women and b) ensure that the standpoints of both black and white women should be represented in interpreting the data. Limitations on funding meant that this worker could only be part-time, for a limited period[4].

Neither of these undertakings was straightforward, and we experienced delays which had some impact on the final results of the study.

Overall permission to observe in county courts may only be given in principle by the Lord Chancellor's Office. Thereafter, the presiding judge may or may not agree to the presence of a researcher. Prior to the Lord Chancellor's consent, individual courts were not empowered to grant access to closed sessions. The process of gaining official permission, although ultimately successful, was extremely slow. The individuals dealt with were courteous and helpful, but the system itself is not designed to allow decisions to be made quickly. Once access was eventually granted, however, in February 1989, there was no difficulty in gaining permission from individual judges to sit in on their court sessions, and, over the period of observation, only one judge, in Bristol County court, declined to allow a researcher to be present.

We initially understood that permission to sit in on magistrates' courts sessions would also be granted centrally, via the Home Office, but this turned out not to be the case. Instead, we had to approach the Magistrates' Courts' Committees for the respective areas, and in each case, permission for an observer to be present was granted readily, to be effective from January (Bristol) or February (Kendal).

With regard to the appointment of the co-researcher, the Research Group appointed a woman in November 1988, but she was unable to take up her post, as (being an Indian citizen) she needed a work permit which the Home Office, after considerable delay, refused to grant her. We subsequently appointed another worker (Anjali) who commenced her employment in June 1989. This delayed start unfortunately meant that she was unable to take part in the court observations (as there was not sufficient time available to obtain permission for her to attend) and her input into the design of the research was also severely limited. She was, however able to spend some mornings in the waiting room of Bristol County Court and make contact with women there. She also interviewed some women and some professional workers in both Bristol and Kendal, and has been able — subject to time constraints — to participate in the data analysis and writing up. Another woman, (Parveen) has also been employed by the project on a sessional basis in order to make contact and undertake interviews with Asian women in their mother tongues.

Implementation of the Research Design:
(i) Court Observations

Once we had obtained permission to observe in court, our next task was to find cases to observe. As regards Bristol County Court, there was no difficulty at all: Friday has been designated "injunction day" and almost all full hearings, and many *ex parte* injunctions and committals for breach come to court on that day. Jackie was therefore regularly present on Friday mornings and usually throughout the day from early February until the end of June. On some Fridays, more than one judge was available to hear injunctions, and in this case, a choice was made between courts according to information given by the court clerks and ushers regarding which cases might be of greatest interest. In general, contested cases, and committal hearings, were preferred to *ex parte* applications, which were typically extremely quick routine procedures about which an outside observer can often gain very little information. Some cases were followed through on several occasions — from the initial *ex parte* application, through the full hearing the following week, to repeated appearances for breach of injunction or undertaking.

In regard to the magistrates' courts and to the courts in Kendal, one major problem was the extremely limited availability of cases to observe. In Bristol, as throughout Avon and several other areas in the south of England, the county courts are almost always preferred by solicitors for matrimonial matters (see Murch *et al.*, 1987), and hence very few

7

personal protection order applications reach the magistrates' courts there. In consequence, there is no regular day set aside for protection order applications. In Kendal, there was no marked preference for either court (though some solicitors had their own personal preferences — see Chapter 6), but protection orders and injunctions were almost non-existent during the period of the study, and when applications did arise, they were often at extremely short notice, so that it was impossible for a researcher to be present. Alternatively, some applications were withdrawn at the last minute, sometimes after the researcher had already travelled to the court concerned. Towards the end of the study, Jackie was able to be present at two protection order hearings in Kendal, and a discussions of the issues raised is included in Chapter 4. Apart from that, the data from court observations relate almost exclusively to Bristol County Court, which we realise may differ in certain important respects from other county courts, and the procedures are obviously different from those of magistrates' courts.

Implementation of the Research Design: (ii) The Sample of Women

As we have said, one important consideration was to talk to a wide spread of women, including particularly those who had not needed or been able to go into a refuge. We tried a number of approaches for making contact. One obvious point of contact was the court itself, and this would have the advantage that we would have both observational and interview data relating to the same woman. After some hesitation, we made tentative approaches to women in the waiting room or as they emerged from the court room, introduced ourselves and explained about our research, and gave them a letter giving more details and with a tear-off slip they could return to us (see Appendix). It was not always easy to make these approaches as the waiting room was typically very crowded with women, men and their respective solicitors and barristers coming in and out and often trying to check affidavits or negotiate agreements between opposing parties. The presence of the woman's abuser was especially inhibiting, so we were unable to make our approaches systematically, but chose women who were sitting by themselves and where a relatively private conversation could take place. Over the five months we were sitting in court, we approached approximately 50 or 60 women, most of whom were initially receptive and friendly, but only six were eventually interviewed.

We do not find this limited response at all surprising. As we will show in detail later — going to court is an extremely disturbing experience, and women who are in the waiting room, or have just had their case heard usually have too many other things on their minds to want to commit themselves to taking part in a research study. One women, interviewed eighteen months after starting legal proceedings, explained:

I think if you'd come when I was actually going through this, it would have been one more thing that I would have found it hard to cope with. And I would have been much less coherent — though I would have remembered the legal aspects better. (51)

We naturally did not wish to add to any woman's distress at such a time, so did not try to persuade anyone who indicated reluctance.Some women nevertheless telephoned us, or returned slips indicating their willingness to be interviewed, and others made an immediate arrangement to see one of us. Even so, keeping these appointments sometimes led to difficulties. In some cases, by the time we called, the woman's circumstances had changed and she was unable to see us; for example there might have been a reconciliation. Alternatively, where a woman had experienced a great deal of trouble, and perhaps recurrent attacks, she was often so weary of the whole business that she had no desire whatsoever to talk to a stranger about it, and we certainly did not wish to add to her pain by pressing her.

Another appropriate means of contact was via a woman's solicitor, and we circulated forty-four solicitors (eight in Cumbria and the rest in Bristol), telling them of our research and including several copies of a letter for them to pass on to women who had recently consulted them regarding domestic violence. (Solicitors were drawn from the Law Society's Regional Directories. Only those solicitors who took legally aided clients and noted matrimonial advice as among their three most common areas of work were contacted.) Thirteen solicitors replied (most of them positively). Three or four seemed to have moved away or were no longer practising. A few solicitors were very helpful, and about six or seven seemed to have passed our letters on to clients, usually with good response. It may be that other solicitors passed on letters but omitted to tell us, and the women themselves decided not to get in touch, but obviously we have no way of knowing this. Overall, we feel that the response from solicitors was disappointing.

In a study of this kind, when researchers are trying to gain access to people who are in the process of going through major changes or crises in their lives, considerable persistence combined with sensitivity and tact is necessary. The concept of "response rate" is not meaningful here, when dozens of letters may need to be distributed to gain one or two positive responses which can be followed up. In spite of the women's widespread — and understandable — reluctance to be interviewed, those women who participated appeared to find it a positive and sometimes therapeutic experience, and we were often able to reassure them or give them information about what was going on, or alternative options they could try.

To augment our sample, we had to make contact with women by other means. we produced a poster which we asked various organisations such as Citizens Advice Bureaux and public libraries to display for us. This was not, however, at all productive, as only two women contacted us, one of whom was looking for a support group rather than offering herself as a research subject. We did talk to a few women who were or had been in refuges. (In addition, two women who contacted us via solicitors were in refuges). We also used personal contact — particularly in the case of Asian women who could not be contacted by any other means. (Although we had our letter translated into Urdu and Punjabi and circulated a large number of Asian and Black women's organisations in Bristol, we have had no response from this.)

We have had particular difficulty in making contact with black women. During the months we were observing in Bristol County Court, only a very few black women made injunction applications and no Asian women at all were seen in either the waiting room or the court room. Our sample therefore includes only one Afro-Caribbean woman from this source, and a further eleven Asian women contacted by other means. The court process is often particularly inappropriate for Asian women, as some of our interviews indicate. (See Chapter 5.)

The number of interviewees could obviously be increased by calling on all those women who had failed to respond to a letter, but whose addresses we knew from sitting in court, or via their solicitors. However, in a study of this nature, concerned with such a sensitive subject, we felt this would have been an unacceptable invasion of privacy. Moreover, in certain circumstances it could have been dangerous — both to the woman and possibly to ourselves — if the violent man had been present in the house at the time of our call. (On two occasions when women had initially agreed to an interview and given us their telephone numbers, the man had answered the phone, having returned home in the meantime. This again is potentially dangerous, and even if the woman had still been willing to be interviewed, we chose to withdraw immediately.)

If a similar study is undertaken again, we would recommend that a much longer time be allowed for making contact with women, using all available sources, including courts, solicitors, social services departments, community organisation, CABx and so on. Some of these letters take time to filter through to their recipients (we were contacted by two women who had heard from their solicitors three months after we sent the letters out, and certainly solicitors with only a small number of clients in this category may need several months to find suitable women to whom to pass on letters) and some women need time to decide they want to reply.

Altogether, we interviewed 31 women[5] (27 in Bristol and the surrounding area, 3 in Cumbria and one from a town in the north.) The majority of these women (19) had recently taken out an injunction or a personal protection order against their partner; nine others had separated, or were in the process of divorce; a very few were still with the violent partner. Of this sample, six women were approached while they were waiting for their case to be heard at a county or magistrates' court. Nine women contacted us after their solicitors had passed on our letters to them. One woman responded to one of our posters advertising for volunteers. Four women were or had been in refuges, and contact was made via Women's Aid workers. Finally, eleven women were already known to one of us before the research began.

Interviews were normally between an hour and a hour and a half in length — the longest lasting four hours. We followed a schedule (included in Appendix) but did not always stick rigidly to the same order of questions, but adapted both the order and the question wording as appropriate, according to the woman's circumstances and particular concerns. We asked to tape-record all interviews, and we later transcribed them in full. The semi-structured and open-ended nature of the questioning meant that the material we obtained was often very rich and extensive, and full of personal detail, but it was not easily susceptible to "objective" comparison and analysis. We do not, however, regard this as a major problem, and the sensitive nature of the subject matter meant that this kind of approach was essential.

Another potential "problem" concerns possible discrepancies between women's subjective accounts and the accounts which might have been offered by other individuals involved — for example, the women's legal advisers or their partners. As Jan Pahl points out, however, "women's accounts are valid in themselves" and "their subjective interpretations ... of their needs and of the solutions... offered to them are crucial" in any assessment of the adequacy of the legislative and social control measures (Pahl, 1985, pp.73 - 84). When, on occasion, we have been able to set the woman's account against those of others, or our own court observations, we have nonetheless put the greatest weight on *her* assessments rather than those of others.

Implementation of Research Design:
(iii) The Professional Workers' Sample

Given the perspective outlined above, we see the interviews we have undertaken with professional workers as complementary rather than the main focus of the study. We therefore made no attempt to interview a representative sample of relevant professionals but chose instead to concentrate on a few individuals — who were mostly sympathetic to our research — in order to illustrate some of the problems from another perspective.

Because the focus of this study is on legal remedies, we felt that the views of solicitors would be of most relevance. We therefore requested interviews with a small number of solicitors (four in Bristol, six in Cumbria) who had experience in matrimonial matters and in injunction/personal protection order applications. This side of the study was particularly important in Cumbria, in view of the limited number of women we were able to interview (none in Kendal itself).

In Cumbria also, because so few women there appeared to be going

11

through the process of injunction applications, and we were unable to contact any, we decided to talk to a rather broader range of professional workers. In this we were guided by the Clerk to the Justices who was extremely helpful in suggesting people whom it would be appropriate to interview. These included: a senior police officer, a probation officer, two local authority social workers, two volunteers from Victims Support, a CAB worker, a magistrate and a worker in a women's refuge. Our objective in these interviews — given the lack of applications to court in during 1989 — was to try to establish the extent and seriousness of domestic violence in the area, the kinds of support and advice that were offered, and some views on what women in the area facing this situation typically do. Because of time constraints, we were unable to undertake an equivalent range of interviews in the Bristol area, though clearly this would also have been a fruitful strategy. We also had personal communications from a judge (outside the areas of study) and a barrister (in Bristol) which have helped us with interpreting the statutory basis of the law.

Overall we believe this study has highlighted a number of areas of concern, while at the same time indicating that in certain limited circumstances the legal remedies may be able to provide effective protection. (Even in such cases, however, the emotional strain of undergoing the court process has to be offset against the relief obtained. Only the woman herself can judge whether the net result was beneficial to her.)

Although we have only looked at Bristol and Cumbria, it is clear that local practices — with regard for example to the choice of courts and legislation and the speed with which applications can be heard, and the availability of suitable alternatives to the legal process — differ widely. Some of these differences may suit local circumstances, and work well (for example, the practice of making appointments at quarter hour intervals in the Kendal magistrates court); others result in unnecessary problems for the women concerned. All are designed primarily with the convenience of the legal personnel in mind, rather than for the benefit of their clients.

The structure of this report is as follows. In *Chapter 2*, we outline the different legal remedies which may be available to women experiencing violence or other abuse from her partner. *Chapters 3 and 4* discuss the legal process as it is experienced by the women themselves. In these two chapters, we draw on data from our court observations and from interviews with women experiencing domestic violence. *Chapter 5* focuses on the experiences of Black (particularly Asian) women. In *Chapter 6*, we present data we collected from our interviews and discussions with the professional workers involved: solicitors, volunteer workers, magistrates, judges, barristers, social workers, police officers and court clerks. (In some cases, there may be only one or two representatives in a category — due to restrictions of funding and timescale). *Chapter 7* summarises our findings and presents recommendations for future research and ·for changes in legal practice. In the *Appendix*, we present further details of our research methodology, including reproducing our interview schedules and other research instruments. A Glossary of legal terms used is also included.

Footnotes

1. A minority of women were experiencing violence from partners who had never lived at the same address, and their experiences are also included. Two women whose cases were observed at court were being abused by teenage sons. We did not come across any cases in which a woman was the abuser. While we are aware of, and sympathetic to, women who experience violence from female partners in lesbian relationships, none of the women we spoke to was experiencing this kind of abuse, and none of the court cases referred to this situation.
2. Sue Gorbing has also conducted a similar study, but it has not yet been published and we have been unable to trace her Master's thesis.
3. Her earlier articles (1977a, and 1977b) were written before the DVMPA had come into effect.
4. Because of limitations on funding and timescale, it was not possible to appoint her for as long as we would have liked. Ideally, the proposal would have been made jointly by black and white women (see p4) or, failing that, both workers would have been full-time and would have started together at the commencement of the study.
5. In one case, by letter only.

CHAPTER 2:
THE STATUTORY BASIS OF THE LAW

Introduction

In this chapter, we are going to be looking in some detail at the legal measures which give the courts power to make orders aimed at protecting individuals from assault, molestation or harassment from an abusive partner. We hope to provide a reasonably concise and clear explanation, for non-lawyers. We anticipate that while a few readers will read this chapter straight through, many will use it for reference purposes, only, and will prefer at this point to go straight to our account of the findings of our research, in Chapter 3 onwards.

The most important forms of protection which are available for a woman who is living with a violent partner are:

1. a non-molestation or protection order aimed at preventing further abuse or harassment.
2. an exclusion or ouster order aimed at removing the man from the house and/or keeping him away, usually for a set period.
3. permanent regulation of the occupation, ownership or tenancy of the joint ("matrimonial") home; this is likely to be associated with permanent separation or divorce.
4. re-housing in temporary or permanent accommodation elsewhere.
5. criminal prosecution of the violent partner.

Our main focus in this study has been on the first two options, though we have been aware that the third and fourth options may, in the long-term, be of most use to women. The option of prosecution may be helpful in certain cases, but it is aimed at punishing the offender rather than protecting the woman, and in practice may put her and her children in further danger.

Three statutes give the courts express power to grant "matrimonial" injunctions or protection orders[1]. These are: the Domestic Violence and Matrimonial Proceedings Act 1976, which applies to the county courts (often referred to simply as the Domestic Violence Act, or DVA); the Domestic Proceedings and Magistrates' Courts Act 1978 (the DPMCA or Magistrates' Courts Act); and — for exclusion and ouster orders, only — the Matrimonial Homes Act 1983. In addition to these statutory powers, the county courts and the High Court have general powers to grant injunctions ancillary to some other remedy within the court's jurisdiction, or in support of a right recognised by general law. These powers are particularly important to women who are still being harassed or assaulted following divorce or separation, or who have never lived with their abusive partners. They were also the *only* means by which women could obtain relief prior to the introduction of the Domestic Violence Act. It is important to note that although the law gives these powers to the courts, they are discretionary, and individual judges and magistrates vary quite widely in the extent to which they exercise their statutory powers.

The Domestic Violence and Matrimonial Proceedings Act, 1976

The Domestic Violence Act was introduced into Parliament as a private members' bill by Jo Richardson in 1976, following on from years of lobbying by the National Women's Aid Federation (as it then was), and in part as a response to the recommendations of the Select Committee on Violence in Marriage, 1974-5. As a private members' bill — albeit with government support — it was subject to certain limitations; in particular, that no expenditure of public money be required for its enforcement, and that it should be straight-forward and non-contentious in order to ensure rapid progress through Parliament. The Act came into force on June 1st 1977.

The Domestic Violence Act made four major changes in the law:

1. It facilitated the procedure for obtaining a non-molestation injunction without the need to start other proceedings (e.g. divorce) at the same time. It was therefore aimed at providing *emergency* protection.
2. Such an injunction could be backed up, when the court believed this to be necessary, by police powers to arrest the man when he broke it. A "power of arrest" could also be attached to a matrimonial injunction made in connection with divorce — but not to other kinds of injunctions or court orders (see below, p18).
3. An exclusion or ouster[2] injunction could also be granted under the same legislation: that is, the violent partner, if still living in the home, could be excluded from it (or from part of it) for a specified period; if he had already left, he could be ordered not to return; and if one partner had left the shared home because of violence or abuse from the other, then she[3] would be allowed to return and he could be ousted. If the court thought such a provision were necessary, the man could also be kept away from a specified area surrounding the matrimonial home, and/or from other specified places, such as the woman's place of work or the children's school.
4. All the provisions were equally available to both married and unmarried couples, provided they were deemed to have been

15

"living with each other in the same household as man and wife" at the time of the assault or abuse. This was the first time that married and unmarried cohabiting women have been treated equally in legislation relating to their relationship or their shared home.

The provision for attaching a power of arrest may be exercised in cases where the judge is satisfied that the defendant has caused actual bodily harm to the applicant or to a child in the household, and that the offence is likely to be repeated. This provision is particularly important, since it means that the police are able to arrest without a warrant if they have cause to believe that the injunction has been broken, whether or not they are satisfied that any other arrestable offence has occurred. For example, where an exclusion order is in force, and this is backed up by powers of arrest, any attempt by the man to enter the property would contravene the order, and could in principle result in an an arrest; whereas an injunction without these added powers would simply allow the police to ask the man to leave. The problem arises, as we shall see (Chapter 4) in practice: not only are the courts reluctant to attach a power of arrest, even when all the statutory conditions apply, but, even when one is in force, the police often fail to exercise their discretionary powers.

When a man is arrested on the power of arrest, he must be brought back to court within 24 hours for his case to be heard. When an injunction without a power of arrest is broken, the onus is on the woman (or her solicitor) to apply to the court to commit the man for contempt of court. In either case, in principle the man may face a prison sentence — *not* for any assault but because he has contravened a court order; but in practice, the court is extremely reluctant to commit unless there have been repeated breaches of an injunction (or undertaking: see below, p21).

As with other legislation, the provisions of this Act have been clarified and modified by case law, and by Practice Directions from the President of the Family Law Division of the High Court (see below, p24). Because of the speed with which the DVA was introduced, there were a number of gaps and ambiguities in it which the courts have had to rectify.

The Domestic Proceedings and Magistrates' Courts Act, 1978

Historically, the matrimonial jurisdiction of the magistrates' courts has evolved in response to a particular concern for the position of working class women (see Law Commission, 1989; McGregor, 1957; Finer, 1974). Magistrates' courts have been seen as cheaper and more accessible to working class women than the county courts or High Court; (though in practice, this may not always be the case.) The DPMCA was aimed at bringing the family law administered by the magistrates' courts in line with that of the divorce courts (with the exception of divorce itself). The provision of protection against domestic violence was one of a number of measures covered in this Act, and was the first to come into force (in 1979.)

The DPMCA allows magistrates to grant personal protection orders and ouster orders in very similar terms to the non-molestation and exclusion injunctions granted by the county court, and powers of arrest may also be attached in appropriate circumstances. There are, however, a number of restrictions which do not apply to the county court legislation:

a) Applicants to the magistrates' courts have to be legally married to the partners against whom they are applying for an order.

b) The magistrates' courts are not empowered to protect against harassment, but only against physical violence. If the man has made threats, but has not, as yet, been physically violent either to his wife or to their children, then only if he has been violent to someone else are his threats taken seriously by the court, and protection granted.

c) Children "of the family" may be protected, but this excludes children simply "living with" the applicant (for example, foster children), who can be protected where appropriate under the county court legislation.

d) Exclusion orders are only allowed on notice, and not under the expedited procedure. In practice, an expedited protection order (i.e. anti-molestation) will be granted, and the exclusion order application will be adjourned till the following month. This severely limits the scope of the magistrates' courts in regard to emergency protection of women and children.

e) The Act does not allow a man to be excluded from an area surrounding the matrimonial home.

The procedure for enforcement, when an order has been breached, also varies in the magistrates' courts, and to some extent may be more satisfactory. Magistrates have power to impose penalties for breach of orders made by their courts, and they can themselves institute these powers. Alternatively, the applicant herself can apply for an arrest warrant (where an order which had no attached powers of arrest has been broken), and if the respondent is arrested as a result, he can be kept in custody, or released on bail, pending proceedings. There are no equivalent powers pending proceedings in county courts, nor can the county court issue an arrest warrant for breach of a civil order.

The Matrimonial Homes Act, 1983

As with the magistrates' courts legislation, this Act applies to married couples only. Under the Matrimonial Homes Act, the county court or High Court has powers to "prohibit, suspend or restrict the right of either spouse to occupy" the matrimonial home, or "require either spouse to permit the exercise by the other of that right" (MHA, ss.1(2)(b) and (c) and 9(1)). There are also powers to restrict or terminate the rights of occupation of a spouse who is not legally entitled to the home. These orders are not, strictly speaking, "injunctions", and are not really intended for emergency protection, but aimed at resolving marital disputes on a more long-term basis. Moreover, it is not clear whether an order made under the MHA would be effective in preventing a violent man from visiting the home, or whether it simply precludes his occupation of it. Nevertheless, in effect, they may act as exclusion orders, and — in the light of the Richards' judgement[4] — when a married woman is applying to exclude her husband from the matrimonial home, the judge, in considering whether or not to grant the order, will apply the criteria of the MHA, whether or not the application is being made under that legislation, or under the DVA.

The criteria to be considered in deciding whether the exclusion of a violent spouse is "just and reasonable" are:
1. the conduct of the spouses in relation to each other and otherwise.
2. the respective needs and financial resources of each spouse.
3. the needs of the children.
4. all the circumstances of the case.

None of these statutory criteria is supposed to be paramount over any other. In particular, the needs of the children are *not* to be regarded as of prime importance, as in some instances, prior to the Richards judgement, had been the case (e.g. Spindlow v. Spindlow, 1978; Rennick v. Rennick, 1977). The effect of this judgement has been to put the emphasis on the man's unacceptable (usually violent) behaviour, and, since Richards, there appears to have been no reported case in the Court of Appeal of an ouster in circumstances other than physical violence (Law Commission, 1979, footnote p.22).

If the originating application is made under the MHA, certain details regarding the title to the land and particulars of any mortgage need to be given. The respondent has eight days within which to acknowledge service, and a further fourteen days to file an affidavit in answer to the application, so the hearing cannot take place for twenty-one days after the original summons. An application to abridge these time limits may be made, but in general this procedure is *not* designed to cope with emergency situations where immediate protection is needed.

Other legislation for obtaining protection

As we have said, it has always been possible to obtain an injunction ancillary to other proceedings, as part of the inherent and general powers of the county courts and the High Court. One way in which this is commonly done is in conjunction with an application for divorce. Such an injunction may have any or all of the features of a matrimonial injunction under the DVA — including the addition of powers of arrest in appropriate circumstances. As we have suggested above, the criteria for obtaining an exclusion injunction are now those of the Matrimonial Homes Act 1983, though the procedure is more straightforward, and only two days notice is required once the man has been served, for the full *inter partes* hearing.

The concept of "domestic" violence seems to imply that the woman and her violent partner are living together within the same home. There are other circumstances, however, in which the violence, though clearly "domestic" in character, stems from outside the home. Such cases include ex-spouses and ex-cohabitants who continue to harass or assault their partners long after they have ceased living together; and boyfriends who have never shared a home with the women they are abusing. In other cases, a father, son, brother or other male relative may be assaulting his daughter, mother, sister, etc. Whether or not these men are living in the same households as the women they are abusing, none of the preceding pieces of legislation applies, and the applicant must use other measures to ensure her protection.

Even after a decree absolute, it seems that the courts still have power to grant a non-molestation injunction (but *not* an exclusion order[5] ancillary to the divorce, provided this is aimed at the protection of the woman and her children. Where the *children* are the main focus for protection, and the couple have never lived together, then the Guardianship of Minors Act, 1971, may be used, but this cannot be used to oust someone who has a right of occupation. The principle purpose of this Act is to determine issues of custody and access, but an injunction to protect both mother and child may be applied for ancillary to those proceedings. Injunctions may also be granted in wardship proceedings, again primarily to protect the children who are the subject of the wardship application.

When non-cohabiting partners or family members other than spouses are the perpetrators of the abuse, an action "in tort" is often the only way to proceed; that is, the injunction application is made ancillary to an action for damages for an offence such as assault or trespass. This is not really appropriate in the context of domestic violence because the main object of the tort system is financial compensation, which is usually neither forthcoming nor desired.

Nevertheless, under the present state of the law, it is all that is available. A further limitation is that all such injunctions may only be granted in support of a legal right; for example, the right not to be assaulted, and the right to exclude others from one's own property. It is *not* therefore possible to specify harassment or molestation within such an injunction, nor is it possible to exclude the offender from an area surrounding the home. If, moreover, the attacker is owner (or part-owner) or (co-)tenant of the property in which the woman lives — as he may well be if, for example, he is her father — it is impossible to exclude him from the home, since in this case, there has been no "trespass" in law. (The injunction can therefore only be made in relation to an assault.)

Injunctions which are obtained in civil proceedings for assault or trespass generally last until the hearing of the civil claim. The injunction is only intended to be an interim measure, pending the hearing, but if no date is set, then effectively the injunction may last indefinitely. The practice now seems to be developing, however, of granting such an injunction for a specified period, after which the claim for damages will lapse if it is not proceeded with, but the applicant is given "liberty to apply" to extend the injunction if she feels that it is still necessary.

If the assailant is a minor — for example, a teenage son — then he will need to be represented in court by a *guardian ad litem*. This frequently leads to considerable delays (as it did in the two cases observed during the course of this study) as, in the absence of an adult relative who is prepared to take the boy's side, an official guardian has to be appointed. Moreover, even when this hurdle has been overcome, the courts are (perhaps understandably) extremely reluctant to exclude a teenager from his home unless every other avenue has already been tried, and the circumstances are clearly exceptional.

One further serious limitation on all injunctions which are obtained in proceedings other than divorce or under the DVA or DPMCA is that they cannot have a power of arrest attached.

Some general points about injunctions and other court orders

Legal Aid

Women who apply for injunctions or protection orders in the courts are usually legally represented, and are often eligible for legal aid to cover their costs (see Chapter 3). Usually they will have a solicitor, and quite often, in the county courts, the solicitor will decide to instruct a barrister as well (see Chapter 6 for a discussion of the factors involved in this decision). The man (i.e. the respondent) may also be legally represented — though quite often he may choose not to be, and in that case, may present his case himself (and will be given some help from court personnel to enable him to do so.)

Although the woman may well be advised to consult a solicitor, and to have legal representation in court, it is important to stress that she *does* have the right to present her own case in court, if she chooses to do so, or if for financial or other reasons, she is unable to instruct a lawyer. In such circumstances, she may find it easier to use the magistrates' court (assuming that she fits the criteria — in particular, that she is legally married to her assailant). This is because firstly, the Clerk to the Justices at the magistrates court is by law obliged to help and advise unrepresented clients, both in making their initial applications, and in presenting their cases in court; and secondly because there is no need for a typed and sworn affidavit (as there is in the county court) since all evidence is presented to the magistrates orally.

Emergency Situations

In an emergency, injunctions under the DVA, in matrimonial proceedings, under the Guardianship of Minors Act, or in tort may be applied for *ex parte*, that is, without the other party being present. This should mean that the woman could be in court the same day or at the latest the next day, if the circumstances warrant it; that is, that the assault is likely to happen again, and she has nowhere safe to go. In the magistrates' court, the emergency procedure is termed an "expedited" application. The magistrates are not empowered to make exclusion orders under the expedited proceedings; and whereas the county court *may* make *ex parte* exclusion orders, they are normally extremely reluctant to do so. Powers of arrest are also very unlikely to be attached *ex parte* in either court.

Undertakings

One practice which is commonly followed in the county courts is to substitute an "undertaking" for a court order. This tends to happen at the second (on notice, or *inter partes*) hearing, when the man or his lawyers suggests to the woman's legal representatives that, although he denies the allegations made in her affidavit, he is prepared to promise or "undertake" not to assault her and/or to leave the matrimonial home by a specified date. This strategy ensures that none of the evidence is heard, and that no judgement is made either way on the truth or falsity of the allegations.

21

If the woman accepts this offer — and almost always she will be advised by her lawyers to agree, since it makes the whole procedure much easier and simpler for them — then her application for an injunction will either be withdrawn or adjourned, and the man will be asked to sign the undertaking instead. (There is no facility in the magistrates' court for making or accepting sworn undertakings.)

In theory, an undertaking which is signed in court has the same force as a court order, and breach of such an undertaking is subject to the same penalties for contempt of court as any other breach. In practice, however, it does not have the same force. Moreover, because the man signs the undertaking willingly, he cannot be subject to a power of arrest. We will explore in Chapter 4 some of the problems which may arise in practice when a woman agrees to accept her partner's undertaking rather than continuing with her application for an injunction.

Serving notice

A different kind of problem occurs when the man disappears shortly after assaulting his partner. This can cause difficulties at two stages: in serving notice on him of the court hearing; and in serving the order on him, once it has been agreed by the court. Some men make a habit of coming and going unpredictably — so that further attacks may occur, but neither the police nor any representatives of the court are able to catch up with him.

If the man has not had the prescribed notice of the full hearing — four days in the case of the DVA, two days for most other proceedings — then the case can only proceed *ex parte*. This means that the order is likely to be made for a limited period (probably a week) only, that the woman will have to return to court yet again when that expires, and that an exclusion order will almost certainly not be granted (even though in theory the county court has powers to do this *ex parte*). It is important to note that the court *does* have the power to rule that "service is deemed good" — if, for example, the woman is prepared to swear on oath that she has told her partner of the hearing date. Courts seem reluctant to take this step, however, until the case has returned to court on several occasions.

No court order has any force until it is served on the person who is subject to it. In most cases, the woman's solicitors arrange for this service, usually employing private detectives to do so; or the court can itself appoint an official to serve the documents on the man. Ideally, the documents are supposed to be served in person: they cannot be delivered through the post. Where the man has, to all intents and purposes, "disappeared", the court may allow "substituted service";

that is, the documents may be served on someone else — such as his mother or a new or former girl friend — whose whereabouts are known, and who is also known to be seeing the man regularly. Again, this is a provision which some solicitors seem unaware of, since they may fail to ask for it on behalf of their clients.

The homelessness legislation

A number of women believe — with good reason — that their partners would not take notice of any court order, however severe the potential sanctions for breaking it might be. In such cases, the homelessness legislation is of more use than the provisions of family law.

The Housing (Homeless Persons) Act 1977 was the first piece of legislation to specify domestic violence as a factor leading to homelessness. This Act has now been incorporated almost unchanged into Part III of the Housing Act 1985.

Under these Acts, a woman is homeless if she has accommodation in which she is entitled to live, but if she does so, she will be at risk of violence or threats of violence from some other person residing there. (Until very recently, threats of violence from someone outside the home, who nonetheless threatened her while she was in it, were not covered by this legislation. However, recent case law has established the principle that women in this situation *should* be eligible for help under the homelessness legislation.) If in addition to being "homeless" under the above definition, she is also "in priority need", then the local authority has a duty not only to give her advice, but to provide accommodation for her immediate needs.

The criteria for being in priority need are specified in S.59 (1) of the Housing Act 1985. These include:
a) she is pregnant
b) she is "a person with whom dependent children reside or might reasonably be expected to reside".
c) she is vulnerable because of old age, disability or handicap.
d) she is homeless because of a natural disaster — such as a flood.

The Code of Guidance which accompanies the Act states that local authorities should consider women *without* children as "vulnerable" if they are at risk of violence. (C.o.G., para.2:12(c)(iii).) It is not clear how many local authorities follow this practice, however.

Generally, in cases of homelessness, a person is expected to present her or himself to the local authority within which s/he has recently been living, or with which s/he has a "local connection". In cases of domestic violence, however, the legislation expressly states that the need for a local connection should be waived if a woman is at risk from

23

further violence if she returns to her home area. A woman should therefore be declared as "homeless" in the authority where she presents herself as such.

An important stipulation is that she should not be regarded as "intentionally homeless". A woman might, for example, be regarded as intentionally homeless if she deliberately relinquished a tenancy before she had received written confirmation from the local authority that she will be offered alternative permanent accommodation. Rent or mortgage arrears, which may lead to eviction, might also be regarded in this light. This should *not* however be a factor to be considered in cases of domestic violence.

Initially, a woman will be offered temporary accommodation, only, while the local authority investigates the situation. Temporary accommodation may be a hostel or a bed and breakfast hotel, or other short term sub-standard accommodation. (Refuges count as temporary accommodation, and therefore women in refuges are still regarded as "homeless" and entitled to re-housing). The woman does *not* have to "prove" her case by obtaining an exclusion or non-molestation order in the courts, and in fact the courts have ruled that to do so, when she has no intention of returning home, is a misuse of court time. (Regina v.Ealing Borough Council *ex parte* Sidhu, 1982; Warwick v. Warwick, 1981).

One situation which may cause problems is where a woman and her partner are joint tenants of an existing council tenancy and are unmarried. Because of the rules relating to security of tenure, the council is unable to repossess the property from the violent man, but if they accept the woman's claim, they also have to re-house her in another place, thus creating two tenancies where one existed before. In a situation of severe housing shortage this is clearly a housing management problem of considerable proportions. Nonetheless, it should not be allowed to stand in the way of the woman and her children being offered alternative, safe, accommodation of their own.

Some councils employ the strategy of the "McGrady notice" in such cases. Since a joint tenancy lapses if *either* party relinquishes it, the council can agree to re-house the woman if she gives up her previous tenancy. A woman should never accept such an offer without taking advice, and without having written confirmation from the council that she will be given a new tenancy.

Developments in case law

After a new statute becomes law, there is a gradual process of clarification and sometimes modification, as particular points of law are tested and taken to appeal. Judges who decide on individual cases in the

Appeal Court, the High Court or the House of Lords can make rulings which then become legally binding on other judges sitting in the lower courts. Rules of law which are set by the House of Lords, which is the highest appeal court, must be followed by all courts dealing with similar cases. Court of Appeal rulings have to be followed in subsequent Court of Appeal cases, and only the House of Lords can over-ride decisions made there. These rulings are called "precedents". Only if the facts of a second case are significantly different from the earlier precedent can the judge "distinguish" and not follow the binding decision.

Precedents set in case law are reported in Law Reports, legal periodicals and in some sections of the national press. Statements on how the law should be interpreted are also published as Practice Directions. A study of both case law and Practice Directions is necessary for a full understanding of how the law is interpreted in practice. Most cases never go beyond the county court level, however, and are therefore not reported. This allows considerable variations in interpretation and practice between different judges in different parts of the country, because most judicial decisions are never tested at appeal.

Case law relating to matrimonial injunctions has centred on three main areas: the rights of unmarried cohabitees; the conditions under which exclusion orders may be granted; and the availability or otherwise of powers of arrest.

Rights of cohabitees

The DVA (though none of the other legislation) was drafted with the intention that it should apply equally to married and unmarried couples, provided they lived together "as husband and wife". Some judges were, however concerned that, if an unmarried woman were allowed to exclude her cohabitee from the house in which they had been living together, this would — assuming that he were either sole or joint owner or tenant of the accommodation — effectively over-ride the man's rights to "his" property. Accordingly, in two cases brought to the Court of Appeal in 1977 (those of B. v. B. and Cantliff v. Jenkins), injunctions previously granted by the county court were discharged on the grounds that the courts had no power to grant exclusion orders in such cases, even though the relationships were of long-standing and there were children involved.

If such a ruling had remained law, one of the major intentions of those introducing the DVA would have been frustrated. However, in the much publicised case of Davis v. Johnson, which went to the House of Lords at the end of 1977, it was ultimately ruled that the Act did give protection to an unmarried woman living with a man in exactly the same way as it did to married women. The power of the courts to exclude a cohabitee who was a joint tenant was therefore upheld — albeit for a limited period only.[6]

Limitations on exclusion orders

Following this ruling, the Appeal Court judge in the case of Hopper v. Hopper (May 1978) reiterated the view that exclusion orders should be granted for a limited period only, "for such reasonable time as will enable the woman to make other arrangements" or, in the case of married couples, to allow a property adjustment order to take take place ((1978) CLY 1596). This recommendation was formalised by a Practice Direction two months later, in which it was stated that "in most cases, a period of up to three months is likely to suffice, at least in the first instance", although the applicant could then apply for an extension if the situation warranted it [7].

A woman's chances of gaining an exclusion order *ex parte* have been progressively limited by a series of cases beginning with Ansah v. Ansah in 1977, where the judge ruled that only an urgent need to protect the applicant and her children, and the impossibility of tracing the respondent made this course of action allowable. A subsequent Practice Direction in June 1978 stated that *ex parte* injunctions (of *any* kind) should only be granted if "there is a real immediate danger of serious injury or irreparable damage". There have been many subsequent occasions when a judge in the High Court or Appeal Court has reiterated the "draconian" nature of ouster orders, and this clearly has the effect of reducing their availability, however deserving the case might be [8]. Certainly an *ex parte* ouster order, where the respondent has rights of residence, and is still living in the matrimonial home, seems to be virtually unheard of in most county courts today.

The Richards Judgement

One case which certainly initially caused considerable reverberations was that of Richards v. Richards ((1983) 2 All ER 807). Mr. and Mrs. Richards lived in council accommodation and had two young children. The wife filed for a divorce on the grounds of her husband's unreasonable behaviour, but remained in the home for some months after this. She then left, taking the children with her, to stay with a friend, and tried to find alternative permanent accommodation for herself and her children. When she failed to find anywhere suitable, she applied for an ouster injunction against her husband. This was granted and the Court of Appeal upheld it on the grounds that the needs of the children were paramount. Mr. Richards then appealed to the House of Lords, and won his case (though in the meantime, the couple had come

26

to an agreement which allowed each of them to occupy the home for part of the week, the children remaining there the whole time.)

The leading judgements were given by Lord Hailsham and Lord Brandon. In reaching their decision, they ruled that the *general* power of the High Court to issue injunctions was now subject to the *particular* criteria of the MHA. Accordingly, they ruled that the court should not treat the interests of the children as paramount, but only as one of several equally significant factors (see p18 above). Lord Brandon also made some points relating to the procedure that should be followed, and this resulted, for a time, in considerable procedural chaos, and a marked drop in injunction applications made ancillary to matrimonial proceedings[9].

There was considerable debate about the effects of this judgement, and various views have been put forward. Maggie Rae and Jenny Levin, in an article in LAG Bulletin (Rae and Levin, 1983) believed that any application for an ouster order by a *married* woman would in future have to be made under the MHA, with all the disadvantages in terms of complexity and delay that this would entail. This was certainly the *immediate* effect in many courts. After the reverberations had passed, however, later commentators tended to disagree with this pessimistic interpretation. For example, Patrick Parkinson (1986) argued that the DVA could and should still be used in emergency situations involving physical violence, but that the MHA was more appropriate as a long-term measure, when different and wider criteria could apply. Now, however, the consensus of opinion among lawyers is that, whichever statute is used, and whether or not the parties are married, the criteria for deciding whether or not to grant the exclusion order should be those specified in the MHA. (Hamilton, 1984; Gardner, 1987). (Our views regarding these criteria are set out in Chapter 7.)

Powers of arrest

The ability to attach police powers of arrest to a matrimonial injunction is one of the major reforms instituted by the DVA. Section 2 (1) of the Act states that these powers may be attached to any injunction containing at least one of the following provisions:
a) restraining the other party from using violence against the applicant
b) restraining the other party from using violence against a child living with the applicant
c) excluding the other party from the matrimonial home, or from a specified area surrounding it.

Such powers are only to be attached if the court is satisfied that the respondent has caused "actual bodily harm" to the applicant, *and* that he is likely to do so again. In all cases, the extent of injury — and not simply the assailant's actions — should be specified in the affidavit. Similar provisions apply to the magistrates' courts legislation, except that the requirement that the respondent has "physically injured" the applicant may be somewhat more stringent. The power of arrest may last for as long as the order itself, or may be restricted to a shorter period only.

The availability of powers of arrest was limited quite early on by the Court of Appeal in the case of Lewis v. Lewis ((1978) 1 All ER 729). The judge in this case ruled that powers of arrest should not be regarded as a "routine remedy" nor should they be granted without giving the respondent notice. This case did, however, establish that judges had the right to attach a power of arrest to any matrimonial injunction, whether it was applied for under the DVA or in the course of divorce proceedings. A subsequent Practice Note ((1981) 1 WLR 27) reiterated that a power of arrest should not be regarded as a routine measure, and advised that a time limit not exceeding 3 months should normally be imposed.

Prosecution

All the preceding pieces of legislation operate within the system of civil law. Prosecution, on the other hand, is a criminal matter. This means that it proceeds through a different set of courts, the standard of proof is higher, and the woman herself is no longer the applicant but is, instead, a witness who can be compelled — if the prosecution decides to proceed — to give evidence against her assailant. This can be a real problem for women who may, in the meantime, have become reconciled — however temporarily — with their partners; or who may have received serious threats either from their attacker or his associates, and therefore have good reasons to fear for their own safety if the case proceeds. (This was the situation experienced by Michelle Renshaw who, in a widely publicised case in 1989, was imprisoned by Judge Pickles for her supposed "contempt of court" because of her fear of giving evidence against the man who had beaten her severely.)

In law, an assault which occasions either actual bodily harm (ABH) or grievous bodily harm (GBH) is a criminal offence, wherever it takes place and whatever the relationship between the assailant and his victim. (Sexual assault is, however, treated differently if the woman is legally married to her attacker: rape in marriage is still not a crime under English law.) As far as the police are concerned, however, a "domestic" assault will result in a charge only if it is perceived as a "serious" one, and only then if they believe that the woman will not withdraw her statement before the case comes to court.

The police no longer have responsibility for prosecutions but must

28

pass each case on to the Crown Prosecution Service, who will decide whether or not to proceed. The CPS employs a filtering procedure whereby cases in which they believe there is little chance of conviction are dropped; this means that domestic violence cases, and cases of rape where the parties are known to each other, tend to be filtered out.

Assuming the case passes through this process, it will then proceed initially to the magistrates' criminal court. The first appearance may be as soon as the following day, but the case will then almost certainly be adjourned for a month or so to allow the prosecution to collect their evidence and the man to prepare his defence. During this period, the man will be remanded, usually on bail, and it is likely that the magistrates will attach conditions to the bail — for example, that he must not contact his wife or return to the matrimonial home.

When the case returns to the magistrates' court, the man will be asked whether he pleads "guilty" or "not guilty". If he pleads "guilty", then no evidence need be called and the most likely outcome, if it is a first offence, is that he will be "bound over to keep the peace" for a period. If, on the other hand, he pleads "not guilty", witnesses (including the women herself) will be called, and, depending on the seriousness of the charges, either the accused or the prosecution may opt to have the case adjourned to the Crown Court to be heard by a judge. Since, following the Police and Criminal Evidence Act 1984, spouses may now be compelled to give evidence against each other, the woman will not usually be able to withdraw once this stage has been reached. If a reconciliation has taken place, or if she is now unwilling to appear for other reasons, she may be termed a "hostile witness" but she will be subpoenaed to appear in court on the appointed day.

It is important to reiterate that, in a criminal prosecution, the woman herself is *not* legally represented, and has no control either over the process of the case or its outcome. The objective of a prosecution is punishment of the offender rather than protection of his victim(s). In some, probably few, cases, it may act as a deterrent to further offences. It may also serve a symbolic function in stressing that violence within the home is as much subject to criminal sanctions as violence outside it; but, while this may well be in the public interest, it will not necessarily impress on each individual man the seriousness of his offence.

Nonetheless, there may be circumstances in which the woman feels that a prosecution may be helpful to her; for example, if she decides to claim compensation for her injuries from the Criminal Injuries Board. If a woman agrees to proceed with a prosecution, or if that decision is taken out of her hands, she should be entitled to co-operation, support, and continued effective protection from the police during and after the trial.

Footnotes

1. For the purposes of this study, the terms "matrimonial" and "marriage" will also apply to cohabiting couples in so-called "common law" marriages, except where otherwise stated. The term "injunction" applies to a court order, obtained in the county court or the high court, aimed at restraining someone from doing something (e.g. assault his wife) or alternatively stipulating that he do it (e.g. vacate a particular property). A "protection order" is an equivalent order obtained in the magistrates' court. In practice, in everyday speech, the terms "injunction" and "court order" are often used interchangeably.
2. Strictly speaking, the term "exclusion" applies to an order which is made after the man has already left the matrimonial home, and confirms that he must stay away from it. An "ouster" order is one in which a man is turned out of the home he is still occupying. Some lawyers argue that the terms apply to different statutes; i.e. "exclusion" order applies to the DVA and "ouster" to the MHA; and that moreover, an ouster order simply terminates or suspends the right to occupy the home, but says nothing about visiting it. However, in both legal parlance and common understanding, the terms tend to be used interchangeably, and that will be the practice within this report.
3. All the laws which are discussed here apply equally to both men and women. For the purposes of this study, however, we will assume that the man is the violent partner, and the woman is applying for protection. As we have stated earlier, this was invariably the case throughout our study.
4. Richards v. Richards (1983) 2 All ER 807. The implications of this case will be discussed later, p26.
5. However, if the home is in her name only, and he has no rights to be there, he can be excluded from it.
6. There is no power to protect furniture or other possessions, however; nor is there any power to prevent an owner-occupier from disposing of the property over the woman's head, if she is simply a cohabitee and has no right of ownership.
7. Practice Direction by the Family Division, July 21st 1978.
8. For example, Summers v. Summers (1986) 1 FLR 343; Wiseman v. Simpson (1988) 1 WLR 35; Shipp v. Shipp (1988) 1 FLR 347; Whitlock v. Whitlock (1989) 1 FLR 208.
9. In 1982, there were 7474 injunction applications under the DVA, 26,428 ancillary to matrimonial proceedings, and 53 applications for orders under s.1 of the MHA. In 1983, the figures were 10,453, 15,051, and 1,071 respectively. This trend continued into 1984, when there were 14,130 under the DVA, 12,097 ancillary to matrimonial proceedings and 1,898 orders under s.1 of the MHA. Comparisons with later years are not possible as the basis for collecting the figures changed. By 1987, the recorded number of applications in matrimonial proceedings had dropped to 3,489, but it seems that methodological considerations which the Lord Chancellor's Department were unable to explain must be responsible for some of this discrepancy. (Lord Chancellor's Department. Judicial Statistics, published annually, HMSO.) See also Appendix

CHAPTER 3:
STARTING THE LEGAL PROCESS

This chapter is mainly based on data from our interviews with women who had experienced physical or mental abuse from their male partners or ex-partners. We explained in the Introduction how we selected a sample of women to interview. We include the interview schedule (which we used as a guide only) in the Appendix. The quotations included in this chapter are taken verbatim from these interview transcripts, though obviously any identifying details have been removed, and where irrelevant material has been cut, this is indicated by three dots... If it has been necessary to add a few words to make the meaning clear, these extra words are included in brackets.

The vast majority of the judiciary are, of course, male, but in one of the areas under study, there is a female judge who regularly hears domestic injunction applications. Approximately half the county court cases we observed appeared before this woman judge, who would be readily identifiable if the personal pronouns "she" and "he" were used. Therefore, in order to preserve anonymity, whenever we refer to the remarks of a particular judge, we have tried to avoid the use of any personal pronouns. When this has been unavoidable, we have used the terms "s/he" and "his/her", in spite of certain reservations against this practice, which can lead to somewhat clumsy expressions at times, and also, perhaps, blur the extent of male dominance within the court room.

Events leading up to taking legal proceedings.

There seems to be a pervasive myth, endorsed by many in the legal professions, that relationships often break down because "people" (usually meaning women) haven't tried hard enough to make them work. A similar misconception persists regarding injunctions and protection orders. On one occasion in court, one of the judges expressed the view that women often took out injunctions for "trivial" reasons; that perhaps the couple had separated, and there was some tension when the man called back to visit the children, and the woman immediately applied for an injunction in retaliation. This "typical" scenario did not, however, accord with our experience, either as researchers or as Women's Aid workers.

Most of the women we talked to had experienced abuse for several years (in one case, more than twenty) before they finally decided to make the break. (This was also the case with a number of the women

31

whose injunction applications were observed in court. When the evidence was given in affidavit form only, however — as it was for *uncontested* cases in the county court — there was usually no way of knowing the duration of violence from court observations only.) Some women had tried repeatedly to separate or to obtain an injunction — and may have succeeded — before being persuaded back into the relationship to have another go at making it work. Initiating divorce proceedings may sometimes have exacerbated matters (and access visits were then frequently the occasion for further abuse) but we did not come across one case where a couple had lived together but the physical violence commenced subsequent to a separation; (in one or two cases, the abuse was primarily or exclusively of an emotional rather than a physical nature; and in one case, the couple had never lived together, and the one serious violent incident was after she had told him their relationship was over.)

One typical pattern was for the abuse to start almost immediately after a couple married or set up house together:

> When we got married, the day we got married, he took me home and said, right, that's it, you're my wife, you're married to me now, you do what I say. (41)
>
> It was so easy just to get married again. But when somebody changes overnight, which is what he did — he pushed me a couple of times so hard that I've fallen... and I know the violence would have got worse. (31)
>
> He's always been quick-tempered, but first of all it wasn't to me or any of the children, it was towards other people... It wasn't to me until 1980, in fact that was when we got married, just after we got married he started. (26)

Other women found that a man who had always been "quick-tempered" gradually became harder to live with, or more irrational.

> He was just getting more and more violent, more attacks with carving knives, mugs, milk bottles, anything. He threw me down a flight of stairs once... (28)
>
> My husband's behaviour deteriorated throughout our three and a half years of marriage, due to his drinking habits. The violence towards other people in the family, friends, and people in pubs was due to him being drunk. He had not, so far, hit the children or myself, but I felt it was just a matter of time before he did. We took a lot of verbal abuse. (36)

In some cases, this increasing violence was associated with drinking, which became progressively worse as the man became increasingly dependent on alcohol. There is a persistent myth that alcohol abuse is a primary cause of male violence. Our view, however, which has been backed up by independent research is that this is a rationalisation which can never justify nor explain the violence (See, for example, Kantor and Strauss, 1987). The excuse that "I was drunk — I couldn't help myself" is hardly an adequate explanation either for the loss of control itself, (it is not acceptable in cases of drunken driving, for instance) or for the consequences; i.e. why do many men (but very few women) appear to "lost control" in that particular way?

In other cases, the woman's growing independence — perhaps getting a job, or going out more as her children grew older or she gained in confidence — seemed to spark off the violence.

> Although he was abusive, very quick temper, quite a lot of shouting ... he wasn't physically violent. That only started when I actually got a job, which changed him dramatically. I don't know why a job seemed to change somebody so much. I started to get my own independence I suppose. (28)
>
> Things weren't too bad when I was at home all day with the children... He hated me going out shopping, but we coped with that... Then we moved here and I started working... I was working longer hours, and then I got another job, and things went from bad to worse. He just resented everything... (21)

Again, this is a pattern which has been noted by other researchers (Gelles, 1972; Homer *et al.*, 1984) and which is open to various interpretations. Certainly the woman's growing independence may seem to challenge the man's authority. This is something that many men — who have grown up with and accepted very "traditional" ideas regarding the roles of husbands and wives — have difficulty in accepting with equanimity. Such men may see physical violence as a sign of "masculinity" and/or as a way of reasserting the authority which they believe is slipping from their grasp.

A third common pattern was a man who periodically became violent for no apparent reason, or as a result of a small incident which would have passed unremarked by many people. Men like this were typically kind, generous and loving in between times, which made it particularly hard for their partners to understand their behaviour, or respond appropriately to their sudden inexplicable explosions.

> He was like a Jekyll and Hyde because one time he could be really good and kind and everything like this and you wouldn't think it was the same person, and the next minute it would only have to be something, little things, you know, and he'd blow up completely. (17)

Even after years of abuse, many women were very reluctant to take any step which might seem to be irrevocable. Although it is possible to take out an injunction for temporary relief without making any decision regarding the long-term future of the relationship, many women were unaware of this, or they did not think it would work; and some solicitors are reluctant, when a woman is married, to apply for an injunction without also initiating divorce proceedings — even though the Domestic Violence and Matrimonial Proceedings Act of 1976 was (among other things) specifically designed for this purpose (see Chapter 2). A woman may therefore have considerable ambivalence about consulting a solicitor, and, as other researchers have shown (Cavanagh, 1978; Dobash and Dobash, 1980) may only do so at a fairly late stage, when she has finally decided the relationship is over.

> I rang up and made an appointment, then I cancelled it, I lost my nerve. I thought, I can't do it, I don't want to talk about it, I don't want to tell anybody... I didn't want to get divorced, I went through the process of those divorces, I actually got divorced but it wasn't what I wanted, I didn't want it, I didn't want those injunctions, I didn't even want to go to the solicitors, I didn't want it this time, but I knew I had to have it. (27)
> I'd made up my mind and there was no going back. As I knew from past experience, it always gets worse, it never gets better, and I'm not going to go through ten years like that again, never. (31)

On this evidence, the view that women take the decision to consult a solicitor "lightly", or take out an injunction for "trivial" or "frivolous" reasons is very far from the truth. Moreover, as we hope to demonstrate in the next chapter, the experience of going to court and the aftermath is, for most women, so unpleasant that even if the initial consultation were made hastily, it seems unlikely that any woman would persist with her case if she could see any alternative way of resolving matters.

Legal Aid

Some women are deterred from getting legal advice because they are afraid they will not be able to afford the cost of consulting a solicitor or going to court. Sometimes, this was because they were did not know about the legal aid system, or did not think they would be eligible. Certainly we encountered women on very low incomes who were expected to pay a contribution towards their legal expenses, and in one case this was a major factor in deciding her against taking out an injunction. More often however, women were eligible for legal aid on income grounds, but had difficulty in obtaining it for other reasons.

> (The solicitor) said he thought it was hopeless and he didn't think the Law Society would grant me the legal aid certificate to get the injunction, but they did. (21) My solicitor never applied for legal aid to cover him in court for custody, so... he didn't get paid for any of that. So I'm sure that's why... he didn't want me to fight for sole custody. (26)

These examples show the importance of the solicitor as gatekeeper to the legal aid system. If he or she does not think the client has an adequate case, then effectively s/he can block any further action. In the second case, the solicitor's failure (through negligence) to apply for legal aid to cover contesting custody meant that the woman had to accept joint custody even though the husband had been violent to the children and the injunction restrained him from molesting them as well as the woman herself.

The legal aid officials themselves can prevent a woman continuing with an action which may be necessary to ensure her comfort or safety.

> (My solicitor) applied for legal aid (for me) twice and they turned it down. I haven't actually got the paper, it was quite technically worded, but all they were saying was, it was too petty to do anything. because he hadn't physically harmed me, but just caused damage, they couldn't do anything, it wasn't worth taking to court. (32)

Several solicitors (who will be quoted in Chapter 6) mentioned occasions when they felt the Legal Aid Board (as it now is) had made the wrong decision on certain cases. One spoke of "capricious" decisions, and others of the lack of consistency between officials, so that depending on the initial letter of the client's surname, legal aid might or might not be granted in almost identical circumstances.

A further problem was the delays which could be caused when the Legal Aid Board refused to grant emergency legal aid, or took a long time in assessing a woman's income. In theory, in emergency circumstances, a case can be brought *ex parte* the same or the following day, the legal aid to cover it having been agreed over the telephone. Sometimes, fortunately, this did happen. Others had to wait to several days or weeks, even for (apparently) *emergency* relief.

> I'd started off the injunction but it had taken quite a while before I got the legal aid certificate through and he was threatening to break in, so I did ring the police and ask them to keep an eye on the house because I was so frightened. (22)

In non-emergency circumstances, if the woman had a job, assessment of her income often took a considerable length of time, such that one solicitor advised his client to give up her job, to make the whole process much simpler. If income was irregular — due to overtime payments, perhaps, or irregular work hours — or a woman had two jobs, or changed jobs, this further complicated matters; and the forms themselves were off-putting and confusing so that some women put off completing them.

If women were not eligible for legal aid, getting an injunction could cost several hundred pounds — more if he evaded service, or if she had to return to court after a breach. It may be cheaper to get a protection order in a magistrates' court, and it may be easier for women to bring their own cases before the magistrates without the need for legal representation (see Chapter 2), though we did not meet any women who had done this. (The Magistrates' Court Clerk we talked to said that he or his staff would always be very willing to advise women about making a personal protection application, and that, in court, it was one of the duties of the clerk to advise unrepresented applicants and respondents in respect of their legal rights.)

Some women on quite low incomes found they had to make a contribution to their legal costs, or even pay the whole cost themselves; and other women were told they would have to pay costs once the matrimonial home was sold. Sometimes the court ruled that these costs had to be claimed back from the man: whereas this practice might deter some men from offending again, others became enraged and women feared they might take out their anger on them. One woman felt quite strongly that it would be "unfair" for her to claim any costs back from her husband, as she was the one who wanted the divorce, and "there is no point in saying 'it was your behaviour' if he doesn't see it that way" (51). Her choice was likely to mean, however, that when the matrimonial home was sold, and her legal fees paid out of her share of the proceeds, she would not have sufficient left to buy another house for herself and the children. She, like many of the women we talked to, was living on Income Support, while her husband had a secure well-paid job.

Seeing a Solicitor

Going to see a solicitor with a view to taking legal proceedings against a husband, boyfriend or ex-partner is, as we have said, a step that many women take reluctantly. One woman told us that she cancelled several appointments before finally deciding to persevere with legal action. For many women, the solicitor's office itself can be very intimidating, and if they have recently suffered a physical assault or other abuse they will be very upset and vulnerable, and may find it hard to explain what their problem is, or take in what is said to them.

> I was sitting there in a complete daze... I just couldn't believe it was happening to me. I just felt I wanted to go to sleep and it would go away. (51)

Women like this, who may have experienced many years of violence and abuse, often lose any sense of self-worth, and their confidence in their own judgements is likely to be severely damaged. This may have implications for their ability to understand legal complexities, or to choose rationally and calmly between the various options which may be open to them. It is therefore very important that solicitors and other legal personnel understand this and try in every way possible to to

36

check that the woman's understanding of her position is adequate, and that she is making the right decisions for herself.

This problem is experienced in particularly acute form by those whose first language is not English, and who therefore may need an interpreter when they attend a solicitor's office. Since few if any solicitors provide this service, women in this situation are dependent on taking a friend or relative with them. In the case of some Asian women, language difficulties may be compounded by cultural differences, which may increase misunderstandings, and mean that the women are less likely to get appropriate advice or protection. Some Asian women are extremely reluctant to consult a solicitor or take professional advice of any kind. If they decide to do so, they may nevertheless find it difficult or impossible to get practical or emotional support from sympathetic friends or relatives, who may prefer not to get involved. (See Chapter 5 for a more extensive discussion of this issue).

Most women will find it difficult, and often shameful, to talk about intimate details of their relationships. Although many television programmes and articles in the media deal with domestic violence, it is still experienced as a very private and personal matter. To open this up to the impersonal professional gaze is an enormous step which requires considerable courage — or sufficient desperation — to take.

It is particularly important that the solicitor be as welcoming and sympathetic as possible, and able to put the client immediately at ease:

> I think it's important to get a solicitor who is going to fight for you because you get terribly worn down and I think it's very easy to give in over things because you are so worn down. (44)

Nine women were very positive about their solicitors, whom they found understanding, helpful and prepared to explain things in simple language to them:

> He's brilliant! He says it in a way that I can understand.... he explains to me what is going on... I thought it was fantastic, you know, someone talks English! I'm pleased, I find him really helpful. (32)
> He's really smashing, he's really understanding, he does all he can... He was there all the time, he was more or less ringing daily to tell me what step was next, and he really was behind me all the way (28)
> I felt sure as soon as I started talking to her that she was going to do something, she was going to help, I'd got somebody who was listening to me and going to help. (23)

On the other hand, an equal number of women had criticisms of their solicitors, for example that they were unsympathetic or did not listen properly, or they failed to explain what was going on.

I found the solicitor very cut and dried, very cold, no compassion, it was just legal. The first time you go to a solicitor's, they should put you at your ease, and I didn't feel at ease. (45)

In a way, he's a bit brisk, he brushes me off a little bit. I do understand and I suppose I do go on a bit, but he's not that helpful. (3)

You've got these men acting as solicitors and it's no use arguing about it, it is a man's world, and I'm not anti-men, don't get me wrong, I'm not — just some of them! But you get them sitting there, so condescending as if to say, "We know your problem, we know what it's all about" and they don't, they don't! (42)

Several women seemed very ambivalent about their solicitors: while describing them as "sympathetic" and "helpful" they nevertheless felt they had not given them enough time to talk things over fully, had not explained things sufficiently, or didn't really understand. This ambivalence is perhaps inevitable, given the situation and the fact that many women felt they most needed moral support or perhaps a counselling approach, which solicitors are usually not in a position to give (and which are in any case precluded by legal aid limitations.) (The solicitors' views on this issue will be outlined in Chapter 6.)

Some solicitors were, however, particularly bad at creating a supportive and sympathetic atmosphere, which would allow a woman to talk freely to them, and trust their judgement. Sometimes, women changed solicitors because they didn't like their general attitude or didn't feel comfortable with them:

I found the legal side of it, the legal advice given by both solicitors was pretty much the same, the only difference was that one was more understanding and compassionate... I think that's quite important. (45)

Feeling at ease with a particular solicitor is very much a personal thing. Some women, for example, felt they could only talk about intimate things (such as physical assault or rape) to a woman solicitor. Others felt equally strongly that they would prefer a man. Not everyone has this choice, however, particularly if they live in a rural area. In Kendal, for example, very few women were practising solicitors (we only came across one, who had arrived in the area very recently) and this must have severely limited many women's choices. New entrants to the profession are now approximately 50% female, so eventually the situation in this respect may improve throughout the country.

Other criticisms are more specific, and perhaps easier to remedy in the short-term, given the will and increased resources. One particular kind of complaint concerned the solicitor's slowness to act. Although recognising that the legal process was often very ponderous and could not be hurried, women found it hard to accept that it might take their solicitor a week to write a letter, or several weeks to set the process of divorce in motion. One woman had waited eighteen months since the decree nisi and still did not know when to expect the decree absolute. Another woman (not interviewed but seen in court) had started divorce proceedings in November and was still waiting in June for an acknowledgement and a court date to be given (a situation which the judge at the return injunction hearing found deplorable).

Whether or not some of these delays could be justified, there were cases where it was clear to us that a solicitor had given completely wrong advice, often with disastrous consequences. One solicitor, for example, advised a woman to agree to sell the matrimonial home, before any consideration of the division of property could come to court. This left her and her children homeless, while her husband was able to obtain another mortgage and a new home on which she then had no legal claim. As a result, she almost lost custody of her children as well. Another woman repeatedly asked her solicitor to apply for interim maintenance on her behalf, but he apparently refused to do so. Several woman were told they had no evidence on which to base an injunction application; this was particularly likely to happen to those women experiencing mental cruelty or harassment rather than repeated or recent physical violence. It is, however, possible to apply successfully for a non-molestation and/or exclusion order in such cases (and subsequently some of these women did obtain injunctions through different solicitors). Some solicitors seem particularly reluctant to advise a woman to apply for a court order against her partner. One woman was told by her solicitor that he must send a warning to her husband before starting the injunction application. In another case, the fact that the police had decided not to prosecute was seen as justification for dropping injunction proceedings as well. It may be that their awareness of the work involved in preparing an injunction application, together with their belief that women may eventually decide not to go through with it, is deterring some solicitors from even offering this option to women.

Women who consult solicitors about domestic violence are often in a particularly vulnerable state and, because of this and their lack of legal knowledge, they have to trust that the advice they are being given is correct. They also need to feel that their solicitor is working *for them*, but so often it seems that the legal process is taken out of their hands, and they feel they have no control over the outcome. This is particularly so once a case comes to court — as we will show later. The practice of solicitors (and sometimes barristers) conferring together without consulting their clients is extremely hurtful and frustrating and many women felt that agreements and compromises worked out in this way — for example, the acceptance of a man's undertaking — were more in the interests of the lawyers than themselves.

The Legal Options

Ideally, having reassured the client, the solicitor should then go on to outline the legal and other remedies which might be appropriate to her situation. When a woman is experiencing domestic violence, these options can include: applying for an injunction or other court order, to prevent assault or molestation, to exclude the man from the home, and/or keep him away from it; going for divorce; or leaving home herself for a refuge or by applying to the local council housing department for temporary accommodation under the homelessness legislation. She may also need to take additional action regarding custody of her children, maintenance for herself and her children, and to secure her long-term housing rights.

In this study, our focus was on injunctions and protection orders and the reasons why or why not women might choose to apply for them. Most women, even before they consulted a solicitor, had heard the term "injunction" — which like many people they used in a very general way to mean any kind of court order — but they were not aware of the different kinds, or the different procedures which could be used. Some women specifically asked their solicitors if they could go straight for an injunction. As we have said, nineteen out of the twenty-nine women interviewed had recently taken out an injunction (eighteen) or personal protection order (one). In one case, this was in response to her husband applying for an injunction against her. Some of the other women had considered applying for a court order but had decided against it.

The main reason women gave for not taking this kind of legal action was that it might precipitate further violence, and possibly reprisals, and that this would exacerbate rather than relieve the situation. Some women who had left their home areas believed that taking legal action would draw attention to themselves and indicate to their abusers where they were now living.

> I were too frightened (to get an injunction) because I was trying to hide because my family was trying to look for me, they were looking for me to bring me back home. (14)

Other women had good reason to doubt the effectiveness of a court order since they had disastrous experiences in the past:

> (Injunctions) always caused me more hassle than been any good. I've always said in the end that I won't take out any more injunctions because they just come up to you with the injunction and say "What's this?" — you know what I mean?... From my past experience with (my first husband) they don't work, they're not worth the paper they're written

on. (41)

Some women applied for court orders against their better judgement, because either their solicitor or the council housing department or homelessness unit was urging this course of action:

> I went to see a solicitor and he said I could go back to my house and my husband should leave the house and I could get an injunction against him. I wasn't very happy about that because I was scared to go back to the house, but I didn't have any choice. (47)

While some councils — for example, Bristol City Council — recognise the limitations of injunctions and accept that their existence is not a valid reason to refuse to rehouse a woman, other councils have a more restrictive policy. There was some indication from our interviews with professional workers in Kendal that the situation whereby a woman is pressured into obtaining an ouster order either so that the council can evade their responsibilities under the homelessness legislation, or in order to "prove" that she has suffered violence, may be becoming increasingly common. (This confirms our experience as Women's Aid workers advising women who are trying to escape from violence at home). This practice may also be of particular significance in rural areas where alternative housing is very limited. It is therefore important to stress that women themselves are usually the best judges of whether or not an injunction will be effective in the case of their particular abuser.

A woman's judgement as to the probable effectiveness of a court order will play a large part in her decision to take that course of action. Her judgement will not always accord with that of her legal advisers. The view of the legal profession that court orders are rarely broken (since relatively few breaches come back to court) ignores the difficulty of enforcing orders effectively: as we shall show later, many solicitors discourage women from pursuing the matter when an order is breached, and many women become disheartened, bitter or terrorised by repeated breaches, which, it seems, everyone is powerless to prevent. Most women simply want the man to stop behaving in a violent or threatening manner towards them. They are often extremely reluctant to be instrumental in sending a man they once loved (and may still care for) and who may be the father of their children, to prison. Consequently, many women themselves decide not to persist with renewed injunction or committal applications. The ways in which the legal system is failing women are, therefore, often invisible, except to those most directly involved.

In the following chapter, we will discuss these issues further, after we have followed women through the process of going to court, and the aftermath.

CHAPTER 4:
THE COURT PROCESS

Introduction

In this chapter, we will be drawing both on interview data, and our court observations which took place between February and September 1989. In order to compare court procedure regarding the granting of injunctions and other court orders, we made attempts to observe proceedings in both magistrates' and county courts in Bristol and Kendal. As cases are heard in Kendal infrequently, however, the majority of court observations have taken place in Bristol.

Overall, we sat in on seventeen sessions (including 172 relevant cases) in Bristol county court, two sessions (3 cases) at Bristol and Northavon magistrates courts, two sessions (2 cases) at Kendal magistrates' court, and one session (one case) on Kendal county court. Thus overwhelmingly, our direct evidence comes from Bristol county court, though interviews with various professionals in Kendal as well as in Bristol (see Chapter 6) have enabled us to make some comparisons in court procedures. We feel that these observations complement our interview data in giving an indication of how the court is experienced by women, and illustrating some of the problems with the legal procedure.

Going to Court

If a woman applies for a court order, she will have to attend at either a magistrates' or county court on at least one and more usually two or more occasions. The first appearance is frequently an *ex parte* (or expedited) one: that is, the other party to the proceedings (i.e. the abusive partner) is not present in court as there has been no time to serve him with notice of the hearing. Because only one side appears, there is no response to the application, which may often seem to be a mere formality.

Courts will only grant ousters or add powers of arrest to an injunction *ex parte* in "exceptional" circumstances, and the magistrates' court is not (at present) allowed to grant expedited exclusion orders under any circumstances. This means that unless the man has already left the house voluntarily, or (less often) has no right to be there in any case, he will almost invariably be allowed to stay in the house until the full *inter partes* hearing.

In the county court, the application is supported by a written affidavit, and at this initial hearing, the woman and her legal representatives will usually be in the court room for only a few minutes while the judge decides whether or not to grant the order. In the magistrates' court, the hearing will take a little longer, as the woman will have to present her case orally. On the first occasion, however, most of the time in court will be spent waiting to go before the judge or the magistrates, since there will usually be no fixed appointment time, but cases will be slotted in according to the convenience of court staff and the demands of other business.

In many courts around the country, including those in our study, the waiting areas are completely inadequate. Sometimes people have to wait in a corridor before their case is heard. Sometimes there is a proper waiting room, but it is often far too small and therefore soon becomes crowded and smoky. Bristol county court for example, is always very busy and this leads to a lot of tension in the waiting room.

> We were there at 10.15 and had to stand, it was so crowded. Apparently all injunctions are heard on Fridays and there were 33 cases to be heard that day!.. We stood all day. There were all sorts of rows going on around us. Young men were being bundled out in handcuffs, children were crying, separated partners were yelling at each other... (36)
>
> We went to court and stood for ages. There didn't seem to be anywhere to sit. We stood on the landing for ages, we were told we probably wouldn't get heard because we were so far up the list or something, we probably wouldn't even get heard that day. We were there for ages, then we got moved to another court... because there was more chance of being heard... It was half past two before we went in. (26)

A basic problem is lack of privacy, and some women particularly resented having to wait in a room with many others all going through similar ordeals. (On the other hand, there were some women who found a shared sisterhood of sympathy in this situation.) There was often a lack of rooms in which people could consult their legal advisers, and we were told of one court in which such consultations frequently took place on the balcony! The length of time people had to wait for their case to be called seemed to be a particular problem in Bristol county court, where most injunction cases are heard on Fridays, and everyone is asked to attend at 10.30 a.m. Cases are then called according to the usher's assessment of the length of time each will take (the shortest and most straightforward cases tend to be heard first).

> We were waiting and it was baking hot... It was in the corridor and I had (been ill) all week and... I hadn't eaten for a week so you can imagine how I felt, and I was there from half ten in the morning till 3 in the afternoon, and it still hadn't gone in. (The solicitor) went to see the usher

and he said, yes, we'll get her in as soon as possible... (32)

I'd been there all day long, one of the last cases to be seen, and I was really all keyed up because I didn't know what to expect. (17)

The sense of urgency is made more immediate when trying to fit emergency applications into a very full schedule. Contested cases, or those which are judged more complicated are usually deferred to the latter part of the day, or even adjourned till the following week. This is very hard on women who may be left with little or no protection over the weekend, when it is also much harder to obtain support from other agencies. Although the courts try to keep space throughout the week for urgent lengthy cases, on several occasions in court, no space was could be found for several weeks, and consequently couples were told to "come back next Friday" when, as the judge remarked, they could probably (after a further long wait) be squeezed into the regular domestic injunction list.

The tension is further exacerbated by the confusion felt by both the women and their lawyers, due to lack of space and time, and last minute changes of judge or court room (or both). One woman's barrister could not be found; and another barrister discovered she was required in two courts at the same time. On two occasions, to our knowledge, women were moved from one court to another, and finally ended up having their cases heard several hours later in another court down the road. If two or more judges are hearing cases that day, then the availability of solicitors and barristers (who may be in several cases in the same morning) is also a consideration.

On one occasion, adding to frustration of women and their lawyers, the usual injunction court was taken by a circuit Chancery judge, who allowed a lengthy business case to be heard before the injunction list. Although this was exceptional, it perhaps reflects the priorities of some judges, and may be more of a problem in other areas where there are no judges whose main interest is in family law. Overall, these time constraints raise the question of how cases should be prioritised, and whether more court time (and more judges) could be made available, or brought in when there is a backlog of cases to be heard.

In the courts in Kendal and in Bristol magistrates' court, the waiting time was usually shorter, but the facilities were even more basic. Refreshments, toilet facilities and a children's play area were either non-existent or were not signposted, and women were afraid to go out and find a cafe in case their cases were called while they were out of the building. Given these conditions, it is extremely important that the court staff — especially those who have a reception function — are courteous, helpful, and reassuring. This was generally the case — *when* such court staff could be found: in two of the magistrates' courts, there seemed to be no one to receive or direct the new arrival, and this could be very distressing to women who did not know where to go, whom to ask or what to do.

If the initial hearing had been *ex parte*, then there was usually a return date which could be anything from a few days to a month later. In the county court, the amount of notice which is needed for the man to attend court — i.e. four days under the Domestic Violence Act and two days when the application is ancillary to divorce — usually allows for the full hearing the following week. Sometimes there are problems, however. If there has been some difficulty in finding the man to effect service, and in consequence the correct notice has not been given, then the judge may decide to grant a further non-molestation order but not an exclusion order, as the man is not seen to have had "right of reply"; and the case is put back for yet another week. Alternatively, however, the judge may decide in spite of the man's absence not to give a return date. This is usually when the man is a cohabitee who has already left the house, and, in the absence of a joint tenancy, has no legal right to return to it. The man is then usually given "liberty to apply" to vary the order, but he would have to pay costs, and if he does not bother and there is no further trouble, the order is allowed to stand for three or six months.

In the magistrates' court, an expedited order commonly lasts for 28 days, which usually gives ample time for the man to be served; but, in the mean time, no exclusion order can be granted, and, unless the man leaves the house voluntarily, the woman is faced with the choice of continuing to live with him, (hoping he takes note of the protection order) or finding somewhere else for herself and her children until the case comes back to court. Since the magistrates' courts can only grant protection orders to married women, both partners have equal rights to the home, regardless of whose name is on the rent book or title deeds.

For the full *inter partes* hearing, the man may attend with or without his legal representatives to give his side of the story. Because of the restricted waiting areas, there is little space to avoid the violent partner, leaving women open to harassment and abuse both inside and outside the court and on. her way there and back home again. Women often found they had to share the waiting room or area with their violent partners, a situation which many found uncomfortable and upsetting, and sometimes potentially dangerous.

> It's got a long corridor and you've got another corridor that leads onto the other corridors, so every time you want to go anywhere you've got to pass each other and it's terrible. That's enough to get you really worked up. I was a total wreck before I even started, before I walked into the court room, just through (husband) being there, and the looking, the looks, and more or less he was mouthing things down the corridor

and it was awful, it was terrible. (28)

It's hard at first, I sat there and he came and sat about 12 feet away and that was very hard. I just wanted to get up and say, let's go into another room. But I made myself sit there, the more I got my confidence back, I thought, well he's not going to touch me, there are too many solicitors about, and if he does, he's being silly to himself. (42)

We had to walk right past him. We sat in the waiting area and we could hear him talking round the corner, every place we moved, he could be seen or heard, which I thought was very bad... (26)

One good thing about Bristol county court was the separate waiting room for only — though the restriction was sometimes ignored (particularly by lawyers) — and to reach it women had to walk through the main waiting area.

If, as some court staff insist, it is impossible to make firm appointments for injunction hearings, even when these are on notice, then the provision of safe, comfortable waiting areas is a priority. Several smaller rooms seem preferable to one or two large ones, allowing for both smoking and non-smoking areas, women-only rooms, and perhaps a children's play area and a refreshment room. Rooms should also be made available for lawyers to have private consultations with their clients.

Inside the Court Room

Once inside the court room, the woman's situation varied according to which court it was, whether or not her partner was present and whether he was challenging her story, or, alternatively, was offering an undertaking to behave himself in future — in which case there was no need for the evidence to be heard.

In the county court, if the man is not contesting the case, then it often goes through very quickly and without the woman herself having to say anything, since most of the evidence is given by affidavit. If, however, there have been incidents since the affidavit has been sworn, or if the man is contesting the order, oral evidence is usually required. In the magistrates' court, in contrast, the woman has to give evidence in court, whether or not her case is challenged. This practice is strongly defended by both magistrates and clerks who believe that they can get a good indication from their stories which party is telling the truth. For the woman involved, however, it is often intimidating to have to talk about such matters in front of at least five or six strangers, as well as her abuser.

Nerve-wracking because I didn't know what they were going to ask me or how it was going to take place... (My solicitor) said, you just generally talk to them as if you're talking to anybody else, and explain your side of the story. (5)

There are emotional as well as practical problems in bringing evidence of domestic violence to court. The hidden and taboo nature of violence within the home makes it very difficult for women to talk about it, and when she is in the witness box and on oath, and talking before a number of people she does not know, these difficulties are compounded. The nature of recording such evidence can be laborious and time-consuming, leading to many silences, and in the confined space of the court room, this can add to the stress. In the county court, the judge will write down any oral evidence verbatim. In the magistrates' court, however, this careful recording of every word is apparently not always necessary, but the clerk tends to record names and addresses accurately and in detail, and then make notes of the salient points which come out in the parties' oral evidence.

Sometimes, lawyers have argued that the added stress of giving oral evidence is justification for the common practice of persuading the man to give and the woman to accept an "undertaking" that he will not assault or molest her in future. (This option is not available in the magistrates' court.) The evidence of this study, however, combined with our personal experience suggests this practice is often undesirable. While an undertaking may seem a relatively unstressful way of dealing with the matter, some women felt frustrated and angry as decisions that concerned them appeared to be made over their heads.

> I couldn't stand up and say what I wanted to say, and I couldn't talk to the judge... You had to convey it all through your solicitor... but when she wasn't conveying what I wanted her to say, I felt really angry...the things I wanted to say didn't come out properly, and I wanted to say other things and couldn't. (17)
> We were actually in court for about 12 minutes and I wasn't even spoken to! The solicitors and barristers sorted things out between themselves... (36)

There are also other problems with undertakings, which avoid some of the difficulties (for lawyers) associated with a contested hearing, but also allow the court to side-step the issues of "truth" and "blame", and may result in a less effective remedy for many women. These issues will be looked at below (p56).

The atmosphere of the court can be frightening even without having to say anything. While most judges, magistrates and court clerks are aware of this and have tried to make domestic courts as informal as possible, they are constrained by the limitations of the setting as well as by procedural requirements. Many courts are held in large dark high-ceilinged wood panelled rooms, with heavy ornate benches and a dais on which the judge or magistrates sit.

> Frightened, shaking like a leaf, I can't stand it. I find it overwhelming

especially in the big court room, it's big and dark and gloomy. I find it quite frightening because it looks as though it's them and you, and you're naughty and you've done wrong, you know... (32)

I hate it, I hate it. I wouldn't mind if I was a solicitor or something, I wouldn't mind that, I'd quite enjoy it, but actually being a witness, it's horrible, it's a horrible feeling, because you feel the guilty one. (31)

In Kendal, the domestic magistrates' court now sits in the Magistrates' Retiring Room rather than in the main court room, and, for family protection hearings, both parties and their solicitors are allowed to remain seated when giving evidence. The same room is also often used for injunction applications before a judge. In Bristol county court, the procedure varies: some cases are heard in an ordinary court room (from which the public are usually excluded), some in a smaller court room, and some literally in the judge's chambers. Both Bristol and Northavon magistrates' courts are newer buildings, which some women found preferable.

Several women mentioned their own feelings of guilt and awe at the court setting. Their partners, on the other hand, seemed mostly to be unimpressed by the legal paraphernalia. There seems to be a difficult balance to be struck between reassuring innocent petitioners while showing rebellious respondents that the court had to be taken seriously. (This point was made by several of the professionals working in this field. Their views will be reported in Chapter 6.)

Whatever the setting, many women were extremely nervous about the whole process. Four of them said that this prevented them understanding what was going on, and a further three mentioned their extreme apprehension beforehand — which was often not relieved by the experience itself.

I was in a daze most of the time. I mean the solicitor took me in... she was the one doing everything, and I was just following like a dazed lamb behind her, not really taking much of it in. (51)

I came out thinking what the hell has gone on in there?... What does this mean? What have we achieved today?... I wouldn't want to go through it again. It's just a nightmare! (50)

Three women said that they themselves felt like criminals:

You feel so helpless. You feel as if you speak or say anything, you'll be slung into jail. It's the whole atmosphere of the thing, you know. (17)

One Sikh woman, who was still living with her violent partner, but hoping eventually to sort out a solution for herself, pointed out that going to court was in itself a stigmatising event, and women who used the legal process were given a bad name in her culture. Moreover, because of her situation, neither a divorce nor an injunction would have been of any use to her. Another woman said she found it hard

48

being the only woman in court. On the other hand, two women whose cases came before a woman judge said they would have preferred a man, as they felt that a woman might be harder on her own sex, and that she must be "very important" and single-minded to have got as far as she had in a male dominated profession.

Most women felt they had had a fair hearing. One woman, however, said that in her experience, some judges were clearly prejudiced; one woman believed that the decision to grant an order or not had already been made before the parties even entered the court room; and one woman was upset that the judge appeared to be suggesting that certain aspects of her affidavit were exaggerated or untrue:

> He was sitting there picking out points in this injunction (sic) and I was in such a fraught state, I thought, how could he sit there picking holes in the thing? He only has to look at me to realise how terrible this is. But you know, "Did he really do this?" and "How bad was it?". I couldn't believe it. (51)

Two other women were angry that their side of the story was not taken sufficiently into account. One of these, whose application came before Bristol magistrates' court, felt that the order she was given — for four weeks protection only — was totally useless as her partner was in hospital and would not be coming home for a month. The other woman, who has also been quoted earlier in this chapter, felt frustrated that the only evidence she was asked to give related to the question of whether or not her husband had alternative accommodation available, and not to his behaviour at all:

> If I thought it would have done any good, I would have stripped off right there and then and said "Look at me, how has this happened?"... but nobody seemed to bother. They made me feel as if I was on trial rather than him, and they didn't say he was wrong or anything... Nobody will let you talk at all! It's just taken out of your hands. (17)

This feeling of having no control over the situation came up many times in different ways and at different stages in the legal process. Ironically, in trying to retrieve some of the power that had been taken from them during years in an oppressive relationship with an abusive partner, women find themselves once more disempowered by the very process aimed at giving them protection.

Injunctions — and their limitations

All of the above points, although very important as far as the woman's experiences are concerned, are perhaps of less significance if as a result, women are obtaining the effective protection they need. But are they? There are three main questions here. Firstly, how likely are women to obtain the kind of order they ask for? Secondly, does the order last for as long as the woman needs it? And thirdly, how effective are injunctions and other court orders in protecting a woman from further abuse? We will look at the first two questions in this section. The third question will be dealt with in more detail in the following section on enforcement.

Our evidence suggests that, whereas virtually everyone was successful in obtaining a non-molestation order or undertaking, anything more than that could be difficult to obtain. Both from court observations and interviews, it was clear that a number of women were unable to obtain exclusion orders, though, in their view, these were essential for their protection. Courts are, perhaps, over-concerned not to deprive a man of "his" home unless it seems absolutely necessary.

> They don't like doing these orders, they just don't like them they don't like putting a man out of his house. Obviously in the end when there's a divorce, one of you has to go ... but to actually make an injunction and say one of these people has to leave home at a certain time, (my solicitor) says they don't like doing it, so they have to be very sure of their facts, weigh everything up. (27)

One judge was heard to remark of one couple, "They've rubbed along in the home for some time. Of course there is some tension but ouster injunctions are remedies of the last resort." Another judge remarked that a woman's application for an ouster was "a bit thin", and refused to grant the order, even though her husband had hit her and her daughter several times. Even in cases where there has been a long history of violence, many lawyers appeared to believe that it would be perfectly possible and safe for the woman to return home once she had an order or undertaking that her partner would not molest her.

Several judges referred to Appeal Court rulings that exclusion orders are "draconian" measures[1], and on several occasions, said explicitly "I can't make an exclusion order *ex parte*" — though this is, in fact, not strictly the case. One judge later explained, "We do it very occasionally but we don't like doing it. Perhaps if she came hobbling in on crutches or something..." and added "It's amazing how these women do cope for a week or a bit longer". On the one observed occasion when an *ex parte* exclusion order was granted, (without the man having already left home voluntarily) there were serious criminal charges pending. This careful concern for the man's "right to reply" sometimes meant that if there had been a delay in service, or if he had been served but failed to turn up on the return date, the case could be adjourned for a further week to give him another chance to state his case.

In other cases, (evident both from the court records and from the interviews) consideration for the man's accommodation needs could lead to his being given several weeks or more to leave home. When a woman had left home while waiting for her case to come to court, the judge seemed more inclined to give the man several weeks to make arrangements to move out, or might even refuse to exclude him at all on the grounds that she clearly had somewhere to go, whereas he did not. (This seemed especially likely if she had left the children behind and there was a custody dispute pending — see below.) In two contested cases, where the woman had formed a relationship with another man, the decision to grant an ouster seemed to hinge on whether or not the woman had "flaunted" her infidelity, the men's lawyers arguing that this mitigated his abuse:

> Barrister for man: Your husband finds it difficult to cope with the fact that you love another man. Woman: I find it difficult to put up with abuse and violence. ...
> Barrister: In many ways, Mrs. Q. has created an intolerable situation, and she has been the author of her own misfortunes, such as they are. She is the one who has met another man and formed a relationship with him... Mr.Q. is frank — he has lost his temper. But he feels he has been provoked. That sort of reaction to the way she has been behaving is not sufficient to ask him to leave the home today.

In both these cases, the parties had been married for a number of years, and the relationships appeared to have been in the process of breaking down *before* the women's new relationships began. Both couples had teenage children who were very disturbed by the new developments, and were taking out their concern on their mothers. Both the women had left home because the situation was intolerable for them, but both wanted to return and to try to build up a stable home life again for their children. In one case, the man was given a month to find alternative accommodation, and in the other — after two lengthy hearings — the exclusion order was refused altogether, and the teenagers remained in the matrimonial home with their father.

When the man has been given time to vacate the property, the woman, while waiting for the exclusion order to take effect, either has to remain in a situation where she may be subject to threats or physical danger, or alternatively go into over-crowded temporary accommodation (such as a refuge or bed and breakfast) until her partner eventually leaves.

> I was asked if I agreed to a leaving date (3 weeks later). This was allowing him three weeks to find somewhere to live. He had plenty of family and friends who could put him up, but he insisted on finding a flat first. Those last three weeks were the hardest. It would have been much easier if it had been with effect from the date of the hearing. The children and I had to watch him gradually moving all his belongings out over the last few weeks. (36)

They gave him a week to get out. I know it doesn't sound a lot when you're under that kind of pressure, you're in one room with the kiddies, and you know that if you put a foot wrong, or anything at all could set him off. And regardless of that piece of paper or anything like that. They might as well have said that he could stay in the house another year as regards that. You know, I really thought they would have moved him out that day. (17)

On the other hand, there were a few women who found that once the order had been granted, things had settled down, even though the man did not move out for a week or so.

I think he was given a couple of weeks to find a flat. He had to be out by a certain day. But I think that was enough. Once the injunction happened, it was enough, he didn't touch me. (51)

Women themselves often know, or can guess, how their partners will react to court orders of this kind. The judge, magistrates or barrister, on the other hand, have no personal knowledge of the man in question, and should be prepared to take account of the woman's understandings and fears.

Courts will be particularly reluctant to exclude the man if there is a custody dispute pending:

When we actually went to court with this, he suddenly looked up and said out of the blue that he was going for custody of the children. So the barrister said there was no way the judge would order him out of the house while there was a dispute over custody... He then straight away once he got his own way, he backed down on going for custody. (26)

On several occasions in court, the judge explicitly rejected the possibility either of making an exclusion order before custody was decided or making an interim custody order before having a welfare report.

Judge: How can I resolve it from my superficial impression today? Whoever has the house has the children... I cannot give anybody sole possession of the house while there is a custody dispute... I wouldn't want to make an interim custody order or jump one way or the other and then find it not borne out by the health visitor or the welfare officer... It seems to me that all the court can do today is to state that both children had better stay living where they are until the custody hearing.

In this case, the mother was in the house with one of the two children, and the father had "snatched" the other and gone to live with his parents. After the parties had left the court, the judge remarked to the clerk, "It's difficult, it's quite impossible. They both come in with completely different stories and when you're dealing with children, it's very difficult." s/he had made no attempt to hear the evidence regarding the alleged abuse, but had recommended cross undertakings because, even if the woman had not done anything wrong, "he will say she has".

In another case, the woman had left and gone into bed and breakfast accommodation with her two children. Because of the conditions in the bed and breakfast place, the children had later returned home, and their mother crossed town twice a day to get them off to school after their father had left for work, and to cook them a meal and stay with them until he returned home in the evening. The following exchange occurred in court:

> Barrister for woman: Both my learned friend (i.e. the man's counsel) and I are worried about what is quite a serious situation. The allegations of violence are denied... This is a serious custody application — applications for custody and ouster. I know your views on making ouster orders while custody is pending. The issue of custody rests on Mrs. X's psychiatric state and her ability to look after her children. There seem to be two possibilities. Either I could say I would like the opportunity to try to convince you that Mrs. X. should have interim custody and you could make the ouster order. Judge: That doesn't necessarily follow! Barrister: Or you could adjourn till the psychiatric report... Mr. X. is pursuing custody and Mrs. X. will not go back to the house. That's not out of cussedness but, having nerved herself to make the break, she doesn't feel she can go back with him there.

The situation was left as it was and the case adjourned until the custody issue could be considered at a pre-trial review several weeks later. This was in spite of the fact that there was some question as to whether the woman would be allowed to stay in her bed and breakfast accommodation — as, without the children, she was no longer "in priority need" under the homelessness legislation.

In a third case, the judge reluctantly allowed an interim custody hearing two weeks later, despite reservations that the welfare reports would not be available then, because the man's barrister argued that "My client has information (regarding his wife's mental state) which would make a speedy hearing imperative".

Occasionally, a woman asked for a man to be excluded not only from the marital home but from an area surrounding it, and sometimes from an area surrounding her workplace and/or the children's school as well. (This is allowed in the county court, but the magistrates' court has no power to grant this kind of order). Such a request usually led to a discussion in court about whether such an order was reasonable or workable; and how could the 100 yard or 50 yard area surrounding the house be delineated? Twice there was reference to a Court of Appeal ruling that such orders were difficult to enforce and should therefore not be allowed. Nevertheless, in three observed cases, such an order was granted.

The courts also seem extremely reluctant to attach a power of arrest to an injunction. As we noted in Chapter 2, this is a consequence of a ruling made in the case of Lewis and Lewis (1978) All ER 729, where the judge stressed that "a power of arrest is not to be regarded as a routine addition to an injunction", and this was reiterated in a subsequent Practice Note. Overall, in England and Wales, just under 30% of orders under the Domestic Violence Act of 1976 and the Domestic Proceedings and Magistrates' Court Act (1978) have a power of arrest attached[2], but this proportion varies between circuits and from year to year. In 1987 (the last year for which we have figures) both in the western circuit (which includes Bristol) and in the northern circuit (including Kendal) the proportion of injunctions awarded under the DVA with a power of arrest was one in four, but in London and the south-east, it was better than one in three, whereas in the north-east, it dropped to one in eight. Among the cases we observed, 23 out of 177 (just under 15%) resulted in an order with a power of arrest attached; (none of these was in the magistrates' courts). This partly reflects the small number of applications for power of arrest (26 in total) but there are many indications that solicitors and barristers tailor their requests to their assessment of the likely outcome (see Chapter 6) and this means that many women, where circumstances warranted a power of arrest, were not achieving them.

There also seems to be considerable inconsistency in regard to the granting of powers of arrest — not only between judges, but even the same judge on the same day can make apparently inconsistent orders. For example, on one morning, unusually, one judge was faced with four applications where power of arrest was requested. In the first case, where there was a considerable degree of violence, and a police prosecution pending, the judge complained that "If we did this with all cases, the police force would drown in a sea of paper", and went on to argue that the man was unlikely to "explode" since he knew about the injunction application but had not bothered to turn up to put his side of the story. After further arguments from the woman's barrister, the judge grudgingly allowed a power of arrest for one month, adding, "I don't think I should be doing it, but I'll give it you for a short period." In the following case, where the level of violence seemed very similar, the same judge granted the power of arrest without demur. The only apparent difference was that the man was present in court. In the third case, the judge completely refused to attach the added powers, on the ground that the man's job was closely connected with the police force; he would, therefore, "know the form", and it was unfair to jeopardise his reputation and career if his court appearance should become known among his police colleagues. In the fourth case, once more, the judge seemed satisfied that the added powers were needed.

On another occasion, the judge suggested to the barrister that a power of arrest — which had *not* been asked for — would be appropriate. This was, however, extremely unusual. Judges in general regard powers of arrest as "exceptional", and certainly not to be used in the case of a first offence, however violent, as the following exchange illustrates:

> Judge: Power of arrest? Solicitor: Yes, your honour. It was quite a nasty assault and she has bruises. Judge: It's a bit of long shot isn't it? Power of arrest when there's no history of this sort of thing. Woman: Excuse me, your honour, there is. Solicitor: In 1984. Judge: Good try! (Power of arrest refused)

When an application is made *ex parte*, a power of arrest is almost never granted, and the woman's lawyers accept this, to the extent of withdrawing the request if the man fails to turn up:

> Barrister for woman: We did ask for power of arrest but I don't think in his absence I can press you for it.
> Judge: As long as he doesn't know her address, one hopes nothing desperate will happen. I'll cross out power of arrest.

The courts try to insist that their authority is recognised and respected, and believe that an order (or undertaking) should be enough in itself, without the need for the extra back-up of a power of arrest. They ignore the reality of the situation, which is that violent men are not generally respectful of the symbolic power of the law. The police, on the other hand, as we shall see later — notwithstanding their actual legal position — frequently insist that only an injunction with a power of arrest is of any use to them.

> Barrister for woman: We would like an order with a power of arrest.
> Judge: Why? Her evidence is that he will take notice of an order because he is in enough trouble already.
> Barrister: Past experience shows that the police aren't willing to get involved unless there is a power of arrest... When my client called the police, they strongly recommended her to get a power of arrest.
> Judge: They always do! (Power of arrest granted reluctantly for four weeks.)

Women themselves are also convinced that a power of arrest is desirable, and feel frustrated that they are not able to get it, particularly if they have been advised by the police that such an order is necessary. Some of them believed, either through personal experience, or because the police had told them this that any "lesser" order was totally useless.

> (Injunctions) are pointless... Other women have had goodness knows how many injunctions and because they're not allowed the right of

55

arrest, they're getting beaten up all the time, so what's the point? .. You lock yourself into your house, you've got no protection from anybody, so you sleep on your settee for a couple of months so that you can hear the window breaking if they climb in, but if you can't afford a phone, what good is it? They won't allow a power of arrest until he's nigh on killed you, and when they get a power of arrest, what happens? They get put inside for 3 months, and you're lucky if they do 4 weeks so what's the point? (42)

Incidentally, several women believed they had a power of arrest on their order when in fact they did not; they mistakenly believed that the little speech some judges (and possibly magistrates, too) tend to make to the erring man — "If you break this order/undertaking, you will be in contempt of court and may be sent to prison" — meant that he could be arrested for any breach. Unfortunately, this was not the case, and, as we shall see below, even when an arrestable offence has been committed, the police are frequently reluctant to do anything about it.

As we have said, both judges and lawyers seem to have an overall preference for undertakings, given "voluntarily", in domestic proceedings. This was evident from our observations in court. For example, judges frequently commended a couple for "behaving sensibly" when the woman had agreed — albeit reluctantly — to accept her partner's undertaking. Quite often, it seemed, a woman's solicitor persuaded her to accept an undertaking because it would make the whole procedure "quicker and easier for all concerned". One woman's barrister remarked in court that "My job is to smooth things over so they don't come back again". In this case, the original application, for non-molestation and exclusion orders with power of arrest attached, was withdrawn and an undertaking substituted. Such undertakings, however, cannot have a power of arrest added, and women are, both for this reason and others, often not satisfied with this approach, especially when their partners have not kept their word previously. They do not believe them to be capable of restraining their behaviour, when there have been long and frequent periods of abuse.

He wanted to give an undertaking. The judge did at one stage want to give him an undertaking, but my solicitor said that he'd been such a pain in the arse, that how the hell could they want him just to have an undertaking? (41)

In some cases, even when the barrister or solicitor argued for an injunction, the judge preferred an undertaking, on the grounds that s/he could only make an order if the allegations could be proved; yet domestic violence is, by nature, hard to prove, as there are usually no witnesses and therefore the onus is on the woman to demonstrate her case conclusively.

Women's dissatisfaction with undertakings and their limitations seem to be ignored by the court. Often women see this as an easy option for their solicitor's benefit rather than their own, and because they are often disregarded by the police, they offer little or no protection if they are breached. This comment is typical of many:

> The police were called actually a couple of weeks ago, when he broke my finger, and the policeman told me that undertaking was not worth the paper it was written on. (26)

The unsatisfactory nature of undertakings is accentuated when one is offered and accepted by the court in circumstances where the man has breached a previous order or undertaking. This happens quite frequently at committal hearings (i.e. when a case has been brought to commit the man to prison for breach of an order) when the woman is nevertheless reluctant — for a variety of reasons, including fear of retribution — for her partner to go to prison, and the court responds to this by suggesting an undertaking. This of course is often weaker than the original order, as no power of arrest can be added, The man himself will feel he has got off lightly, and will take this as an indication of the ineffectiveness of the court.

In one case witnessed in the county court, the barrister — mistakenly — argued strongly for an undertaking with power of arrest, and took some persuading that this was unobtainable in law. He argued, very oddly, that "in this sort of case, an undertaking seems to have more power" because of the "element of voluntariness" involved; yet all parties appeared to believe that the man was often not in control of his actions. Nonetheless, the result was an undertaking — minus, of course, the power of arrest — rather than an order to which those added powers could, justifiably, have been attached.

Even less desirable than a straightforward undertaking by the man are cases in which — in order, apparently, to keep the peace, and be "fair" between the parties when there has been no attempt to assess the competing evidence — the lawyers propose and the court accepts "cross undertakings", or undertakings by both parties that they will not molest or otherwise interfere with each other. This happened to two of our interviewees and was observed in court on nine further occasions, and it was usually apparent that — if there had been *any* molestation on the woman's part (and usually there had not been) — this had been solely for purposes of self-protection:

> Nobody talked to me about (the undertaking) at all. Not even my own solicitor talked to me about it, nobody said anything to me until we were in court... I said to (the solicitor), "Why should I have to take this undertaking?" and she said to me, "Shh!, it's all right, it's all right anyway because you won't do anything" but I felt that wasn't the point... I. had been made to feel — it's like admitting to a crime you

haven't committed to say, well, you're not going to do it anyway so it doesn't matter". (17)

There is some inconsistency among judges regarding the way they approach undertakings. Sometimes they will put a great deal of emphasis on the power of undertakings, and will spell out exactly what the man can and cannot do. Some judges are realistic as to whether or not a man will be able to restrain himself, and will refuse to accept an undertaking if they have doubts:

> Judge: If I take this affidavit at face value, is Mr. Z. going to be able to restrain himself according to this undertaking? ... The reason I raise this is that I had a case recently in which an undertaking was breached, and the man said he was very sorry but he could not help himself. And I believed him. But that does undermine the basis on which undertakings are given.

One judge regularly made a point of telling men that "this promise is being made to me, and through me, to the court. If you break it, your wife will be upset, but more importantly, the court will be upset and that could lead to nasty consequences." Another judge stressed that an undertaking is "a very serious matter" such that even minor breaches should result in sanctions, because ignoring them "encourages a sloppy attitude". We would endorse these comments.

One other occasions, however, when other judges were sitting, men have left the court without even having a copy of their signed undertaking. This may be a mistaken response to pressures on court time: although most solicitors come provided with draft orders or undertakings, these sometimes have to be amended, and then taken away for copies to be made, while the parties concerned remain in the courtroom. In one case, the judge accepted an undertaking offered via the solicitors, though the man himself was not present in court. S/he queried the woman's reluctance to accept the undertaking, saying, "Why are you not protected?... If he doesn't keep to the undertaking, you can have him committed in the usual way" — ignoring all the problems and delays that would entail; (see below, "Enforcing court orders".)

There seems to be an implicit contradiction whereby a man in signing an undertaking implicitly denies any previous assault: no evidence is heard and there is no charge against him, hence his "innocence". The following self-contradictory comment was typical:

> Solicitor: I should just like to say on Mr. P-'s behalf — he would like to say that the allegations are *strongly* denied. He is happy to give the undertaking on the grounds that nothing like this happened and of course it won't happen again because it never did happen.

Judges, too, often made a point of saying to the man that in signing an undertaking, he was admitting nothing and would not in any way prejudice his case at any subsequent hearing. Despite such disclaimers — and bearing in mind that some men might just want to get the business over with in the easiest possible way — nevertheless the fact that the man was apparently willing to agree to an undertaking seems to imply an acceptance of guilt.

In almost all cases, orders and undertakings were time-limited, for three months or less commonly six months or (in the county courts) until divorce was finalised. This was a cause of some concern to many women, and their concern was not without foundation. One woman's husband moved back in when her injunction expired, and she did not think she could do anything about it. Several women did not realise there was an expiry date, and were then taken by surprise when their partners started harassing them again, and taunting them that there was nothing they could do about it.

> I didn't realise (the injunction) only lasted until I got divorced, I didn't realise that it ran out when I got divorced, that it was only temporary... I don't think they should run out, I don't think they should put a time limit on it... Some blokes will do it over and over again, plague a woman's life out. It just doesn't seem to be fair. You shouldn't have to go through that all the time. (32)

From our court observations, we noticed that several divorced husbands were still returning to assault and molest their ex-wives. One husband, whose wife had divorced him several years previously, stated explicitly in court that, "She's my wife, till death do us part, and I must be allowed to go and see her." For both women and men, the legal ending of a marriage does not always signify the emotional ending of the relationship; yet after the decree absolute has gone through, it appears to be much harder to get a further injunction, and there are certain limitations on the kinds of orders which can be granted (see Chapter 2 and below, p122). One woman was actually told by different solicitors, on several occasions, that because she and her husband were now divorced, there was nothing whatsoever she could do about his behaviour — which included battering on her door late at night, and driving his car over her front lawn. This was, of course, not true, and she finally obtained an effective injunction in connection with an action for damages.

Custody and Access Arrangements

Although not part of the injunction hearing, arrangements for custody and access are frequently mentioned, and may determine the kind of order which is made. We have already said that judges tend to refuse to exclude a violent husband from the home if custody, care and control are being disputed. Many judges strongly believe that children need to see and maintain a relationship with both parents whenever possible. They also have a belief in the over-riding importance of the mother-child bond. This belief is widespread in our culture, and has been popularised during the post-war period, partly as a result of the work of John Bowlby and James Robertson and, later encouraged by the explosion of popular books on child care; for example, by Penelope Leach and Hugh Jolly (Leach, 1988; Jolly, 1985). This means that judges and other lawyers tend to assume, when there are no contra-indications, that day to day care and control will go to the mother, but with the father having regular access, and perhaps being consulted about decisions regarding the child's upbringing.

In spite of this assumption — or perhaps because of it — whenever a man challenges his wife's right to have the children living with her, his claims are taken extremely seriously, to the extent of delaying a decision regarding an ouster order (as we have seen above, p52). The thinking seems to be that "everyone agrees that, other things being equal, young children are better off with their mothers; therefore this man's request for care and control must be looked at carefully because he must have a good reason for making it". Judges are, of course, also very concerned that their decisions be *seen* to be fair and gender-neutral; yet as Phyllis Chesler has argued, it requires very little participation for a man to be seen as a good, even an exceptional, father; whereas a woman, conversely, may be judged a "bad mother" on grounds that have little or nothing to do with her maternal abilities (Chesler, 1986).

One example of this is when a woman has left home without taking her children with her — notwithstanding the reasons which may have induced her to take this step. Some judges are inclined to see this as inappropriate, "unnatural", or selfish behaviour, and are less likely to look favourably on her subsequent application to return to the home and/or have custody. Men, on the other hand, are treated much more leniently if they behave in a similar fashion (usually with less justification) since the assumption appears to be that if they make *any* attempt to see their children, they are "caring fathers".

Joint custody orders — though usually with the mother having care and control — are favoured in many cases; in this way, both parents have a say in determining issues such as the education a child will receive, where s/he is to live, and the religion s/he is to be brought up in. "Reasonable" access for the non-caring parent is almost always recommended, and women who challenge this (where, for example, a man has abused his children, or is likely to abduct them) have a very hard time trying to prove their case. "Does he really need to be restrained from molesting his children?" asked one judge — notwithstanding evidence that he had already done so. And a woman who had stopped access after she discovered her ex-husband was allowing their 8 year old son to watch violent and pornographic videos — which gave him nightmares — was reprimanded, and access reinstated. Even when couples were not married, and the man strictly speaking had no automatic right to custody or access, judges seemed uneasy at any suggestion that the children might be better off without seeing their father.

Courts also commend couples who are able to make their own arrangements for their children; (a practice which is endorsed in the recent Children Act). For example:

> Judge: I do think highly of this couple. They're lucky children. If parents can't live amicably together, the next best thing is to agree amicably about the children. Parents are doing this more often now, and when it happens, I really respect them.

While it is obviously better if couples can make custody and access arrangements amicably, this presupposes an element of reasonableness which may not be present in cases of domestic violence. Because of the abuse and intimidation which the woman will have suffered over a long period, she will often be unable to stand up to her husband's demands — yet this may not be evident to the welfare officers and conciliation workers, who may be taken in by the man's superficial charm and articulate presentation of his case.

A particularly worrying feature of some custody disputes is when the man accuses his wife of mental instability such that she is incapable of looking after the children. In many cases, this "instability" — which may manifest itself as depression or extreme anxiety — is itself the result of years of abuse which has totally sapped her self-confidence; however, once away from her husband and building an independent life for herself, she will usually be perfectly capable of caring for her children well. There is also some evidence to suggest that violence to a partner and abuse of a child are related more often than would occur by chance, and that a woman's fears for her children are therefore not unfounded.

Some judges also like to believe that a high proportion of violent incidents are caused by the man's trying to see his children in cases where access arrangements have not yet been made. Certainly, disagreements may flare up around children, and handing them over before and after access visits provide occasions for renewed contact and conflict, but in our view, access itself was rarely the central or originating issue. Sometimes, it may help if a third party collects and returns the children to the home, or if a public place such as a shopping centre is specified as the location for the hand-over; though such arrangements may be fraught, if one party fails to turn up as arranged, or if the third party becomes weary of the task.

We would like to stress once more that women themselves usually know their own partners very well, and if they are concerned about potential abuse or abduction, and request supervised access (or no access at all) their views should be taken very seriously. Some men use the custody issue to force their wives' hand; for example, one man in the study said he would drop his custody application if his wife agreed to sell the matrimonial home immediately, and another applied for custody simply to delay the ouster application. Other men have forced their wives back home by refusing to let them take the children with them when they go. A large (and apparently growing) number of children have been snatched from their custodial parents and taken abroad out of the jurisdiction of British law. Such a situation, which causes enormous distress and sometimes danger to the children involved, is clearly unjust and should be avoided at all costs.

Welfare officers can have a lot of power in determining custody and access disputes, and in almost all cases, judges act on the welfare officer's recommendations. (Exceptionally, in one case we observed, the judge objected to "staying access" — i.e. overnight — for a baby of 3 months, saying it was inappropriate for such a young child. This, of course, reflects the common judicial view that mothers are the appropriate and "natural" caretakers of small children.) Some women felt that the welfare officer was biased towards the man's viewpoint, perhaps favouring reconciliation (if that was what he wanted) and not taking the woman's wishes into account when trying to arrive at some compromise solution. They also felt that their accounts of the abuse they had suffered were not taken seriously, and one woman told us that the welfare officer she had seen, and who subsequently visited her husband, told him her address despite her request that her whereabouts should remain a secret.

Some welfare officers do take on a conciliatory (as opposed to reconciliatory) function, but arguably this should be separated from their other role of providing unbiased reports to enable the court to decide the arrangements for the children. In some areas, including Bristol, there is an independent conciliation service, use of whose services is often recommended to divorcing or separating couples. Conciliation is aimed at arriving at an "agreed" settlement on contested issues, such as custody, access, occupation of the matrimonial home, and sometimes financial arrangements or even the divorce/separation itself. Although such services have their uses, we have reservations about the assumptions of "equal blame" and "communication breakdown" on which it seems they are founded, and there is some dispute as to whether conciliation, in aiming for a spurious "neutrality", merely tends to reinforce pre-existing power differentials (for example between men and women in our society), and thereby favour the man's interests (Bottomley, 1985; Davis and Roberts, 1988, 1989). Moreover, many women have such (justifiable) fear of their violent partners that the thought of having to meet them face to face, even with others present, is utterly abhorrent to them.

Court Procedure

There are a number of indications that judges and other court personnel regard procedural requirements as more important than a woman's safety. For example, in one case, where there had been frequent breaches, one committal hearing was dismissed and another adjourned because of "technical irregularities". In another case, the judge, in effect, sent the woman home to get beaten up again, in order that the man could be arrested on the power of arrest — which would, apparently, have made the whole thing rather more straightforward. In a third case, where an inexperienced judge had attached a power of arrest that extended beyond the life of the order, thereby invalidating it, the more experienced judge at the return date remarked, "What a good job we haven't had any breaches and he hasn't been arrested!" The potential for wrongful arrest would therefore seem to have been more to be deplored than the woman's lack of protection.

At other times, both judges and barristers made clear their total lack of understanding for the woman's position. For example, against the evidence of frequent breaches, a lawyer will make the remark, "You have an undertaking, you're protected now and can go back home". Their concern not to deprive a man of "his" home often seems excessive. We have already mentioned judges' habit of remarking that they "could not" make an *ex parte* exclusion order, implying the law did not allow this (which is not the case). In one case, where an injunction with a power of arrest had been issued the previous week, but the police had delayed arresting the man (after a series of incidents, including threatening his wife and child with an axe, beating down her front door, and throwing bricks through the windows) until a day or so later, the barrister argued that "in the somewhat strange circumstances of this case, perhaps your honour would take a lenient approach today". Another man's solicitor used the lack of correct procedure to argue against the application, and suggested that costs should even be paid by the applicant! The judge refused to accept this argument in its entirety (and did not award costs) but said that certain procedural irregularities should *not* "be put in the way of this couple

63

solving their difficulties". Nevertheless the hearing was adjourned until Monday, by which time at least a legible and correctly worded copy of the application could be issued. The judge added that if this unexpected time had not come free, s/he would have dismissed the application and expected the woman to apply again.

One particular judge was a real stickler for procedural niceties, and accompanied all judgements with a comment on how the procedure *should* have been carried out. For example, in contrast to other judges, (who always seemed pleased when women asked to withdraw applications to commit) this judge pointed out that technically only the court itself had the power to withdraw such an application, once made. s/he also stressed that all evidence should be in affidavit form, and that this should include not only details of the abusive acts, but also of the injuries sustained. This judge favoured a particular wording on all injunctions, reading this out slowly so that the solicitors could copy it down, and objected to any reference to "otherwise interfere with" or "communicate with", which were often standard on orders made by other judges:

> Solicitor: Should we add "interfering"? Judge: Why? What sort of interfering do you mean? If he interferes with her in order to molest her, that is covered in 1). If he interferes to prevent her entering the property, that is covered in 2). And if he interferes to prevent her removing her possessions, that's covered in 3). The great thing is not to use vague terms if we can avoid it. Sometimes it is necessary to use "interfere" but I don't see that it is in this case. It has become a non-word, just used to buttress "molest". The word "molest" is useful in domestic violent cases — we can't use it in other circumstances often, since "molestation" is not a tort, but it is useful in these cases, but it loses its meaning if it is always buttressed by "interfere".

Similar stipulations have been made by Judge Nigel Fricker in his article outlining the standard injunction and undertaking forms used by the north eastern court circuit. (Fricker, 1988b).

This concern for procedure meant that sometimes there was a need to check exactly what the statutory provision allowed. We have already mentioned the uncertainty that one one occasion was expressed regarding the possibility of adding powers of arrest to an undertaking. Another judge queried whether the court could add powers of arrest if the violence had been directed more to the applicant's new boy friend than the woman herself. (This was finally allowed). In another case, where the couple had been divorced for several years, the judge asked what powers the court had after the decree absolute. The barrister explained that "you can't make ouster orders, but in regard to molestation, it's set out very clearly". The judge then pointed out — and the barrister agreed — that the court had no power to add powers of arrest after decree absolute, "but in any case I wouldn't do it *ex parte*, so that really is a non-event."

It was around the question of committal proceedings that judges were particularly concerned to get all the details correct. This will be looked at in the next section.

Enforcing Court Orders

So are court orders effective? Contrary to the view of many in the legal profession, court orders of this kind are only really effective in a limited number of cases. Half the women in our study who had obtained injunctions, protection orders or undertakings, told us that their partners had disobeyed the order or undertaking on at least one occasion. Some of these incidents were relatively trivial — for example, an angry remark when returning children from access visits — though nonetheless threatening. In other cases, breaches of the orders were serious and repeated, but neither the police nor the courts themselves seemed able to do anything about it.

> He's threatened me a few times. I rang my solicitor. He was just turning up, he and the woman he lives with. He's not supposed to come here unless he rings first. The last time it happened, I just came in and shut the door, and rang my solicitor, and said I wanted it stopped. I don't know if he did anything though. (26)
>
> It was all sorts of things he did inside the house to make things difficult. Horrible things like — this is going to sound really badly — like in the bathroom, S.H.I.T. all over the towels and round the toilet, and things like that because I would have to clean it before I could let the children use it. (17)

The effectiveness of injunctions, protection orders and undertakings rests on three things. Firstly the extent to which the man is prepared to respect the (mainly symbolic) power of the law. Secondly, on the actions of the police; and thirdly on the actions of the courts themselves. Unfortunately, if the first of these sanctions is ineffective, neither the police nor the courts, in our view, seem to provide adequate back-up to enforce the orders which have been made. As a result, women have to suffer the consequences of repeated breaches and in many cases living in continual fear for their lives.

> Just more or less he pushed me around a bit, hit me, (the order) got broken, but, I don't know, I think you need to go down with a split lip, black eye, something that's really showing, because they're not bothered about bruises... I went straight to my solicitor, or phoned him, so they'd send him letters warning him if he does it again, he'll go back to court. Interviewer: How often did that happen? At least a dozen times. Interviewer: But you never went back to court? No, because my solicitor felt there was not enough to put in front of a judge. (28)

(The injunction) has actually run out. Not that it did me any good when I had it. When I had that injunction, he actually came to my house and broke my finger, assaulted me and I ended up with a broken finger... He's continuously threatening me. I was going to come to real bad harm, but it wasn't him that was going to do it, somebody was going to do it for him. And you know even my solicitor advised me not to be on my own outside in the dark at any time... (26)

The same day I got my injunction, he was up here and I got hit around. I told the police... and they just said, "Let her go" — because he had hold of both my arms, and I was bruised and everything, and I said, "What are you going to do?" and they said, "Nothing. We'll just let him go." But I said, "I've got an injunction, I've just been to court" and they said, "No, we haven't seen nothing happen". (22)

The last remark quoted demonstrates very clearly the attitude of many police officers: that injunctions are "domestic" matters and none of their business. Nevertheless, most of the women we interviewed had called on their help, often many times, because there was literally no-one else to turn to. The police are available throughout the year, twenty-four hours a day, when most other voluntary and statutory agencies are not; therefore we feel that it is important that they look carefully at the kind of service they provide.

Almost all the comments women made about police actions and attitudes were critical. Five women said the police had told them there was "nothing they could do" when their partners threatened or abused them, and three others said that when they contacted the police after receiving verbal threats, they were told, in effect, to "wait until he does something". Two women felt that the officers who arrived at their homes had treated them in a patronising and offensive manner. For example:

I was very upset, and I had bruises, but he said, "Well, you can't prove it... I don't know that you haven't done it to yourself... Really it was a total waste of time. I have found that most police men side with the man. In fact, one of them actually said to me, "If I had a home like this, I wouldn't want to be thrown out of it, either". (44)

One woman, who called the police late one night when her husband had just attacked her, had to wait till the following afternoon for a visit from them, by which time everything was, on the surface, calm, but she feared that the visit would enflame the situation again:

At three o'clock the next afternoon, there was a knock at the door and there were two police officers standing there. I opened the door and said, "What do you want?" They said, "Are you all right?" I said, "GO AWAY" and just at that moment the back door went and he came in and said, "Who's that?"... If he had seen them, he would have gone absolutely berserk. (42)

There were also a few examples of effective police action. One officer, for example, was quick to arrest one violent man and remove him from the house, and he was in court next day. His bail conditions forbade him to contact his wife — and the police officer called round several times in the next few weeks to check that all was well. Other officers advised women to go into a refuge — and sometimes took them there. But overall, we feel that the police response leaves much to be desired.

As we pointed out earlier, the police will often advise women to "get an injunction with powers of arrest" as they claim that, without that adjunct, they can do nothing. The police *do* however have the power to arrest anyone — whether or not he is the spouse or cohabitee of the victim — for assault, for breach of the peace, or on various other grounds, which would be present in almost all such cases. In addition, many police forces (including Avon) have Force Orders which recommend that domestic violence should be taken seriously[3], and which advise, for example, removing the assailant from the premises, arresting if there are grounds for believing an offence has been committed, and advising and supporting the women and children involved. These Force Orders are, however, usually internal documents which are confidential to serving police officers, and to our knowledge there has been no independent or systematic monitoring of their effectiveness.

Nonetheless, there is considerable indirect evidence from our study that, despite the existence of these Force Orders, many officers display a flagrant disregard for the recommendations. There also seems to be enormous inconsistency between police officers, which clearly adds to the problems women face. Our impressions from our study in no way counteract the results of earlier studies (most of which took place before the recent changes of official policy in many police forces throughout the country) which have highlighted many problems in police practices in this area (Stanko, 1989; Faragher, 1985; Edwards, 1986a, 1986b, 1989; Hanmer *et al.,* 1989; Pahl, 1982; Torgbor, 1989.) It is possible that, where there is an established Domestic Violence Unit within the police force, this may lead to considerable improvements in police practices.

Even when a power of arrest is in force, the police sometimes seem strangely reluctant to act on it. On two occasions in court, police disregard for the power of arrest clause on the order caused the judge to make some strong criticisms of the officers concerned. For example:

> Judge: The only matter which worries me here is the attitude of the police. They seem to have taken the wrong time to act. It's strange how

different police stations take different views. I wouldn't like the police to think that if I overlook it this once, they won't jump to it if there is another breach... I wouldn't want the police to think I don't take this seriously.

In both these cases, the woman's solicitor had contacted the police to find out why nothing had been done, and on one occasion this resulted in a belated arrest. In a further case, in telling her story to the court, the woman explained that, "The police came in but said they couldn't arrest him because it would wind him up, but that I should leave for my own safety."

In spite of our reservations, which stem from the fact that the arrest powers are always left to the officers' discretion rather than being mandatory, there is no doubt that to have a power of arrest attached to an injunction may be an added protection which many women would welcome.

Whether or not such powers are added, if an order or an undertaking is breached, and the woman wishes to do something about this, this requires a further attendance in court, usually for a committal hearing. (In the magistrates' courts, the procedure is rather different, but as we did not attend any such cases, nor did any of our interviewees experience them, we will confine ourselves here to explaining the county court procedure.) The procedure for committal applications is rather complex and time-consuming and all the details have to be strictly adhered to. (See Fricker, 1988a, for a run-down of the correct procedure). Specific instances of all the alleged breaches and their contravention of the original order or undertaking have to be listed on the notice of the hearing, which has to be served on the man in good time to allow him to attend the court. One judge remarked to a clerk when the court was empty, "The powers that be don't understand all the work that is involved in a committal, or the work that is involved when you send someone to prison. If you get a committal order wrong, he can be released from prison."

If a man has been arrested on a power of arrest, the procedure is slightly simpler (see below for one judge's comments) though in such circumstances, the case has to be brought to court within twenty-four hours, leaving the woman little time to collect evidence or muster her witnesses.

Committal hearings are heard in open court — presumably so that justice can be seen to be done — but this can add to the woman's distress, when she is called to give evidence, and is often subject to cross examination. The bailiffs are present at the back of the court room, and often — to save time — the parties in the next case(s) have been called in as well. We witnessed nineteen committal hearings, and a further thirteen cases in which *ex parte* orders had been breached before the full hearing, but although in almost every case the breach was either admitted or proved, only three men were sent to prison as a result. (All three had offended and been back to court on several previous occasions before they were finally committed.) In one case, the first committal was dismissed because of a formality. When this case came back to court for the second committal hearing (after three serious breaches) the prescribed form had not been used and the case was adjourned for a week. At this third hearing, once again the solicitor responsible had failed to include all the incidents in sufficient detail, and the judge remarked "One ought to particularise. I'm quite satisfied that he's in breach of the order, but in his absence (from court) perhaps you would make a note of that". The man was finally committed to prison for 6 weeks, which in itself is an indication of the extent of his violence up to that date.

On a number of occasions, the women themselves stated that they did not wish their partners to go to prison, and requested leave to withdraw their application; this was always granted. Other applications resulted in a reprimand, and a request for an apology from the man, who might then be allowed to offer a further undertaking not to offend again; if this was not forthcoming, a power of arrest might be added to the original order, or a suspended committal issued.

Most judges were very explicit about their strong reluctance to send a man to prison for breach of a domestic injunction or undertaking. For example:

> Judge: Family matters are full of tension and everybody gets jumpy about these things, but you gave a promise to behave in a gentlemanly way to your wife, and if you break that promise, you are liable to be sent to prison. You should bear in mind that your feelings for your child could lead to indiscretions you wouldn't normally have contemplated, and the chance of a flare-up is very likely in the absence of control on both sides. (Committal dismissed but original undertaking is reiterated)
> Judge (to woman's barrister): Don't think I'm not sympathetic to your client — I am — but they will have to be at some stage in this world together. (After repeated serious breaches of previous injunctions with power of arrest, the judge merely ordered that the original injunction continue.)

In one case where the man had forced his way into the woman's flat and there was evidence of severe and unprovoked violence continuing throughout the previous bank holiday weekend, the judge, though accepting both that the man had inflicted actual bodily harm on the woman and her teenage son, and that he was likely to do so again, refused the committal because of technical irregularities and in the hope that next time he would be arrested on the power of arrest because "the paperwork is so much easier"! This conclusion was, it seems, partly based on the judge's assessment of the woman as "strong enough" to endure a further attack, and having "supportive neighbours" (though she was without a telephone and therefore would be unable to summon help quickly.) This is yet another example of judges' concern for procedural niceties rather than the woman's safety.

In our view, this concern for the man's liberty is misplaced and leads exactly to the situation that most judges wish to prevent; i.e. contempt of court. While insisting on the sanctity of court orders, judges nonetheless appear willing to ignore repeated breaches if the man is prepared to "purge his contempt" by apologising. Most men in this situation feel they have "got off lightly", and many of them, as judges, barristers and solicitors all acknowledge, are capable of "playing the system" by continuing with their abuse up to (but rarely beyond) the point where a committal is inevitable.

We should also bear in mind that a high proportion of breaches never come before the courts at all, since they are weeded out either by the woman's reluctance to "tell tales" or her solicitor's insistence that "we must write him a letter warning him first". It is therefore quite clear that, if they are so minded, men can blatantly ignore court orders for a very long time before the law eventually catches up with them. Not surprisingly, women become exhausted and fed up long before this; and some of them, tragically, have been murdered or permanently injured before they obtain effective protection.

Prosecution

Any assault which causes actual bodily harm is technically a crime for which the police are entitled to prosecute. The fact that an assailant may be married or cohabiting with his victim is no defence in law. The majority of women we spoke to, and those whose cases were observed in the (civil) courts had suffered ABH, often many times, yet in only a small minority of instances was a prosecution pending.

There have been a number of studies which demonstrate the reluctance of both the police and the Crown Prosecution Service to pursue the prosecution process in cases of domestic assault; (for example, Sanders, 1988; Bourlet, 1988; Edwards, 1985; Pahl, 1982). This seems to stem from several related reasons: police unwillingness to "interfere between husband and wife"; the belief (which is not always well-founded; see Wasoff, 1982) that women will withdraw the charge before the case comes to court; and the difficulty of getting adequate proof to obtain a "guilty" verdict. Coleman and Bottomley (1976) point out that "the police have their own working conception of 'crime', which is rather different from that held by members of the public" (p.345). Certain offences, including domestic assaults, tend to be "no-crimed" and therefore expunged from police records after the original report has been noted. Because of these beliefs and practices, women are often asked by the police, not once but many times, "Are you sure you want to go through with it?" Given the long delays before such cases come to court (six months in each of the cases we know about) there is ample time for a woman to change her mind.

> The police were obviously concerned because of it being a domestic as to whether I would still take it to court and appear as a witness because if I drop the charges they've got nothing... I think my biggest problem has been the delay in getting through the courts, the prosecution. That's the biggest problem because of the emotional stress it causes. (31)

Although technically it is the Crown Prosecution Service which brings the charges, men often blamed their partners for taking this "drastic" step, and sometimes threatened violence if they did not drop the case.

> I took him to court. I had threats for that, to drop that, from Mike. And I did try. It got so bad that I did try to drop them because I was frightened, but the police said, "It's nothing to do with you, we're taking him to court, you're not, you can't drop them". So I had to go to court. (31)

Many women regarded prosecution as irrelevant to them. They simply wanted protection: they had no interest in punishing their partners. (None of the women we interviewed was taking her case to the Criminal Injuries Board for compensation for the assault, though if any had wanted to do so, a successful prosecution would have been the normal pre-requisite.) One woman, however, who could not afford to take civil action of any kind, believed that the "bindover" she eventually received had the same effect, at no (financial) cost to herself:

> I felt totally and utterly emotionally demoralised and physically demoralised and it (prosecution) was the most effective form protection for me at that time... (3)

The fact that the police have initiated the prosecution process sometimes seemed to help a woman's case when she was applying for an order in the civil courts. This was, perhaps, seen as an indication that the allegations had some basis in fact, since the police were taking them seriously. Moreover, in Bristol county court, at any rate, the fact that a man might be on bail under the condition that he not contact his wife or children was *not* seen as sufficient reason for refusing a court order — as it apparently is in some courts in other parts of the country (personal communication). As several barristers pointed out, neither the civil courts nor the woman herself has any control over the prosecution

71

process; and if the man returned to court and had his bail conditions lifted, then there would be nothing to stop him going home again immediately.

After the case: Long-term housing

Exclusion orders under the Domestic Violence Act are generally regarded in law as emergency remedies to protect the applicant and her children from immediate abuse. Normally they are time-limited, for three or six months. Similar emergency orders in conjunction with matrimonial proceedings usually last either three or six months or until the decree absolute, by which time division of property and occupation of the matrimonial home can be decided. Where a couple is not married, however, but share a tenancy in joint names, the matter cannot be decided so easily. The court generally has no power simply to transfer the tenancy to one of the parties alone; nor — since the provisions in the Housing Act of 1987 regarding security of tenure — does the local authority. In cases of relationship breakdown, this situation creates a problem, not only for individuals concerned, but also for the local authority, which is usually reluctant to offer the woman an alternative tenancy — thus creating two tenancies where there was one before — without the assurance that the man will relinquish *his* claim to the original accommodation.

Sometimes this dilemma has been solved by an agreement between the woman and the local authority, whereby she gives up her part of the tenancy (thus terminating the joint tenancy agreement) on the promise of alternative accommodation in her sole name. This, however, is only possible if the local authority co-operates, and should never be attempted without written confirmation from them, as otherwise the woman could be deemed "intentionally homeless" and left with nowhere to live at all. It also means that she has to have somewhere else to live — for example, a refuge or a bed and breakfast place — while the arrangements are being made, and this can take some time.

Because of this, the injunction courts are often used for what some see as "housing" problems, rather than simply protection and short-term safety. In one case we observed, the barristers acting for both sides insisted that the contested ouster application was "really a housing matter". The judge, however, while accepting this interpretation, argued that "that's what all these cases are about" and decided the issue, in the woman's favour, on the basis of the parties' conduct and their respective needs:

> Judge: I have to consider the conduct of both parties. I cannot see why a young woman should have to put up with this kind of conduct... As far as the needs of the parties, both need accommodation, and the case is

mostly about who should occupy the flat.

Although the order was made for six months only, this would give the council time to sort out a permanent solution to the woman's housing needs.

Less satisfactory was a case we heard about from one of the solicitors we interviewed. Again, the couple were unmarried and had a child, and the man had been persistently abusive, for which the woman had obtained a series of court orders against him. Each time, however, he had moved back in when the order expired, saying it was still his tenancy, and the local authority claimed they were powerless to evict him, and refused even to give the woman and her child temporary accommodation on the grounds that she "had accommodation" she could occupy.

Clearly there are problems when security of tenure (which is in principle desirable) comes into conflict with the equally reasonable wish to live separately from an ex-partner after the relationship has broken down. Ideally, such issues should be decided by agreement between the local authority and the parties concerned; but where this is impossible, as is increasingly likely in a situation of housing shortage, either the council or the courts need to have the power to decide long-term housing rights just as they do in the case of a married couple who are divorcing. Additionally, it may be desirable for certain kinds of conduct, including physical violence and racial harassment, to be grounds for termination of a tenancy.

Conclusion

So what was the overall verdict of the women we talked to on the legal process? Most of them found it very stressful, and the often lengthy delays and repeated court appearances exacerbated this problem. Some women were afraid to use the legal system at all for fear of reprisals or because they had used it in the past to no avail. Some women, on the other hand, achieved exactly what they wanted:

> Peace of mind. Self-respect. My confidence back... Now it's just time to go on with — today, tomorrow, and the new future. the story has really ended now, and I'm glad it has. (27)

> In my own case, the granting of an injunction has given us all the necessary "breathing space" that we all needed so badly. There was no other possible way I could get my husband to leave the matrimonial home... The injunction has given us all a sense of security. (36)

These women were, however, in the minority. Some women — even though they apparently achieved the peace they desired, still felt that the whole procedure had been so harrowing that they wished they had never embarked upon it.

73

I think they're a waste of time... My injunction runs out in September and if he takes notice of that, he can just come back and start all over again, so what's the point of having three months break? (45)

In my case, the injunction did frighten my husband sufficiently for him not to be violent, not to start anything — but it was all on the surface, he was very very angry, and verbally abusive. You could see he was dying to hit me again... He just felt I'd destroyed his life, taken him away from his children. (51)

Others found that their court orders had no effect at all:

No use whatsoever. Even the police man said it wasn't worth the paper it was written on. It didn't protect me at all, and it took all day in court to get it. (26)

I have to say that I think the court system is, at the end of the day, only a piece of paper. And though it is very easy in theory... it just doesn't work like that. (44)

I thought it was an utter waste of time... I thought it was all going to dramatically stop. I think everybody does that that goes in for it, thinks it will all stop. I just couldn't be bothered to go through it again because it is harrowing. (28)

Our evidence shows that when a man is determined and continues to abuse his partner (often for years) there is very little that the slow and formal process of the law can do to prevent it. We believe, however, that court orders could and should be both effective and worth while, without any major changes in the law itself, if the lack of understanding, lack of facilities, and inadequate responses from the legal and professional personnel could be overcome.

At present, however, even when the legal remedies are eventually effective, the length of time the process takes is the cause of much stress and in some cases actual hardship. In our study, this was particularly in evidence when a man decided to contest the injunction or some other aspect of the legal process, such as custody, or divorce. Shortage of court time meant that a contested hearing might have to be put off for several weeks and, when custody was an issue, often welfare reports were called for, and these had to be completed before even the temporary occupation of the matrimonial home could be decided. This is an issue we shall return to later, since it seems to be a particularly worrying feature of some domestic violence cases. Although the adjournment is called for in the interests of "justice" and "the welfare of the child", we believe that no one (save possibly the violent man) gains from this delay, and that there are better ways of ensuring both a fair hearing and a relatively stable home life for the children.

In the final chapter, we will be making suggestions for improvements, not so much in the law itself, but in its implementation. Here, we simply wish to point out that improved facilities in the courts, a speedy and sympathetic hearing, and a *rapid* and effective response from the police, solicitors and the courts, whenever an order is breached, could go a long way to help improve the current situation. None of these reforms would require a change in the law. If judges and magistrates wish their orders to be taken seriously, they should insist that those who disobey them should be immediately and effectively sanctioned. "Provocation" or "losing control" when distressed at the break-up of a relationship is not an adequate defence, nor should it take priority over the protection of women and children from violence within their own homes.

Footnotes

1. Burke v. Burke (1987) 2 FLR 71; Summers v. Summers (1987) *The Times* May 19; Reid v. Reid (1985) 15 Fam. Law 4.
2. Because of unexplained discrepancies in the statistics, and the absence of data, it is not possible to give proportions for injunctions with power of arrest ancillary to matrimonial proceedings.
3. Alan Bourlet, in a study carried out in 1985-6, found that nine police forces have specific policies for domestic violence and a further twenty-four have policies for dealing with breach of injunctions. (Bourlet, 1988) It is likely that, by now, several more forces will have developed such policies.

CHAPTER 5:
BLACK WOMEN AND DOMESTIC VIOLENCE

Introduction

At the outset of the research, we were determined that the experiences of both black and white women should be included. Previous research in this field has failed to consider explicitly the particular position of black women; nor, until the recent publication of the report from the London Race and Housing Research Unit had any study focused specifically on women from African, Asian or Caribbean backgrounds (Mama, 1989).

As Amina Mama points out, domestic violence occurs in both black and white communities and in all creeds, cultures and classes. There is no evidence to suggest that black women are either more or less at risk of violence from their male partners. The violence may have a culturally specific context — for example, both Muslim and Rastafarian men may use their religion to assert their patriarchal authority; but other men simply use their power regardless of any outside source of "legitimation" (Mama, *op. cit.,* p.85).

In black communities, however, the issue of domestic violence has been a particularly sensitive one. Black women are even more reluctant than white women to seek help from the authorities, as, in a racist society, this is often regarded by their own communities as an act of betrayal (Mama, *op. cit.,* p.85). Moreover, black women have less reason even than white women to expect that the law will be on their side. They, like their partners, will have repeatedly experienced racism from the white society. In their dealings with statutory and voluntary agencies they may often have met with hostility and suspicion: they are likely to have been offered the worst housing (or none at all); they may have been asked for their passports before being given medical treatment; sometimes they have been branded as "scroungers" when they have tried to claim benefits to which they are entitled; and many of them have been on the receiving end of police brutality. Shortage of available accommodation has meant that black women often have to share their homes with people with whom they would not choose to live. The consequent over-crowding and other tensions will tend to exacerbate any problems within their personal relationships. (Mama, *op. cit.,* p.21 and passim.[1])

76

Black women in the sample

The particular reluctance of black women to use the legal system to help them gain protection from abusive partners posed considerable problems for our research. One of our main means of contacting women was via the courts, but during the observation period, only three black women (all Afro-Caribbean) were seen to bring their cases to court. We approached two of these for interviews, and both initially agreed, but only one of them was happy to continue when we made contact later. The third woman was approached via her solicitor, but in view of the multiple problems she was undergoing at the time, we decided not to ask her for an interview. None of the women whose names were passed on to us by solicitors was black. The names of two black women only (both Asian) were passed on to us via women's refuges.

We therefore looked to other ways to make contact with black women. Early in 1989, we wrote to approximately thirty community groups in Bristol, many of them defining themselves as for either black or Asian women. We explained our research and asked if they would be prepared to help us in any way. In particular, we asked if they might be able to draw the attention of appropriate women in their organisations to the existence of our project, and ask them to get in touch with us if they would be willing to talk to us. We also had our contact letter translated into Urdu and Punjabi to facilitate making contact with women for whom they were the mother tongues. We had intended that when a black researcher was appointed, she would be responsible for following up these initial contacts, as we believed on the basis of published research (Wilson, 1984; Mama, 1989) and what black women had told us, that many of the organisations we had approached would not feel able to talk freely about these sensitive issues to a white woman. Unfortunately, due to delays in the recruitment process which were outside our control (see Chapter 1, p7) by the time a co-researcher was appointed, there was little time to follow up these contacts consistently, and we did not obtain any interviewees by this method. Accordingly, we were highly reliant on personal contact in order to include some black women in our sample.

In this context, it is interesting to note that the LRHRU team also circulated black women's organisations and community groups in London with information regarding their study, and followed these up with personal visits. Nevertheless, they were forced to draw most of their sample from refuges, which they acknowledge is a "highly select tip of the iceberg" of all women experiencing domestic violence. Our strategy of trying to avoid reliance on refuges meant that we often found it hard to make contact with women at all. This was particularly so in regard to black women, because of the factors detailed at the beginning of this chapter. We strongly believe, however, that a properly funded study, with a much longer time span, and employing black researchers from a variety of ethnic origins, would be able to overcome at least some of these difficulties and could therefore draw an appropriate sample.

In view of these difficulties, the material for this chapter has been drawn solely from interviews with eleven Asian women[2], the majority of whom (nine) were interviewed in their mother tongues by one of our Asian researchers, who had had previous contact with them. (It is important to note that material from these interviews, as well as from the one interview we were able to achieve with an Afro-Caribbean woman, is included in previous chapters also.) We have considerable misgivings about the unbalanced nature of our sample, which we would stress was largely due to the very limited resources which were available to the project. We hope, nonetheless, that our failure in this respect will enable other women to undertake more satisfactory explorations of these issues in future studies.

Asian women: Seeking help

The steps leading to consultation with a solicitor or taking legal action to protect themselves from abuse are traumatic for all women. For Asian women, however, there are particular difficulties, varying with different cultures, circumstances and upbringings. All but one of the Asian women we talked to were first generation women, born in India, Pakistan or Bangladesh, and came over here as young adults, often with their marital partners. To leave the country and culture that you have been brought up in is very difficult. It is also difficult to transplant those values, attitudes and customs into an unwelcoming and foreign country, and it may be more difficult for their communities either to provide traditional forms of support or to develop in different ways as they would have at home.

In their home countries, many women would normally look to their own families for advice and support, if their marriages ran into difficulties. Often both families would get involved, and, if the man was behaving badly, he would be warned that he should change his ways. If that was not effective, then separation would often be accepted as the only possible course. When coming to England, however, women often had no older family members in the country, and were either reluctant to approach in-laws, or felt that they would not be sympathetic or understanding of their problems. Parita Trivedi points out that:

Within a marriage, it is not just the relationship that the Asian woman has to her husband that is the source of tension and inequality. The relationship of the woman to her husband's parents, brothers, sisters, lends a totally different dimension to the kind of force and violence she experiences. Add to this that she may not have any life of her own in this country, or support... (Trivedi, 1984, p.48)

In these circumstances, an Asian woman who needs help will often go to her doctor or health visitor as a first step. Most women, especially if they have young children, will have seen their doctors and other health professionals regularly and will have learnt to trust them. Going to the doctor's is also seen as "acceptable", whereas going to a solicitor or an advice agency is clearly stepping outside customary patterns of behaviour (and is therefore liable to questioning and sanctions, by husbands and in-laws.) It would be particularly helpful for women in this situation if a variety of services (such as social workers, Women's Aid workers and legal and welfare rights advice services) could be provided at health centres and in doctors' surgeries on a regular or occasional basis.

Language

One of the major difficulties for many women is the language barrier. With one exception (the Asian woman who was born and went to school in Britain) the women we talked to either spoke very little English, or felt more at ease in their mother tongues. This meant that, like many Asian women, they had very restricted access to information about the services and resources available to them:

I didn't get enough help because of my language problems. (34)
I need an Asian social worker but it is very difficult to find one. (38)
I speak very little English. My social worker always brings someone with her to communicate. (48)
I think the solicitor was very helpful to me but they should have their own interpreter... I am going to see the solicitor again but I have to find someone who can go with me. (40)

These comments illustrate a lack of interpreters, Asian workers, and support networks. Even when interpreters are available, the service is often inadequate. If a woman needs to consult different agencies — for example, social services and housing departments, as well as a solicitor — she would feel more comfortable having the same woman to interpret for her throughout, and perhaps accompanying her to court if necessary. It takes time to build up trust and feel able to talk freely, and women will feel happier if they do not have to tell their stories all over again unnecessarily. In some areas, health centres have link worker schemes which provide interpreting facilities, but only to aid communication with other health workers. There may also be community interpreting services, but they are not always securely funded, and interpreters may not be available when needed, or a woman may need to accept whoever is free on a particular day, rather than see the same individual she has seen on previous occasions.

This lack of appropriate provision leaves the woman dependent on her immediate circle of friends and relatives to advise and interpret for her if they can, and are available and willing to do so. Several women asked their British born children to come with them when they consulted solicitors, social workers and other professionals. For the children, this situation, in which they were asked to become directly involved in their parents' marital difficulties, could be particularly distressing, and the existence of such close ties could lead to biased interpretations. Sometimes, also, family members and friends refused to help as they did not want to take the side of one party, or perhaps did not agree with the woman's actions.

> I wanted to see my solicitor, but this time I can't because my friend was moved from Bristol. I went to another friend but they don't like to get involved in my kind of case, so I left my problem as it is. I feel the solicitor should have an interpreter. (38)
> I went to the solicitor and saw the secretary. She asked me a few things which I couldn't understand. I only said to her that I wanted to see the solicitor. She asked me my name and address. I felt it was not worth while seeing the solicitor on my own because I can't speak English, so I came back with my son who could speak English, but he didn't want to come with me. (38)
> I am going to the solicitor again, but I have to find someone who can go with me to the solicitor. (40)

These constraints disempower a woman who has herself come to a decision to try to take control of her domestic situation, but is unable to do so because she is crucially reliant on others who may see the situation differently. In this way, both the attitudes of others and the gaps in the service provision combine to deter Asian women from exercising their rights and choices.

Financial Dependence

In Asian families — as in many white families — the family income will usually be dealt with by the male members of the household (Homer, *et al.,* 1984; Pahl, 1989, 1990)[3]. Language again makes it difficult for Asian women to take on paid work, unless they are employed in the family business. Such work as they can do is often extremely poorly paid, and some employers are notorious for exploiting Asian women workers who are desperate for a vestige of independence.

Financial dependence and lack of knowledge of where to go for an alternative income obviously makes it harder for a woman to leave home, especially if there are children. Our interviews demonstrated the lack of control women often had over their finances, and some women were reliant upon very small incomes.

> He did not pay any money for food. When I asked him for money, he started a row, so I gave up asking for money from him because I was scared of him... My Child Benefit was spent on food and I used to get food on credit because I went to an Asian shop near to my house. (47)

> I wanted to leave my husband because he was treating me very badly. I have no money to feed my children. He keeps the money for himself. When I ask for money, he starts to make trouble with me. He says I should manage on the Child Benefit money. The Child Benefit is not enough to run the house. (49)

> If he brings anything for my children to eat, he says, "Your children eat everything I bring home. So next time I am not going to bring anything". Since that time, he has not given me money. I have to pay the bills from the Child Benefit because the house is in my name. (33)

These difficulties were often exacerbated by unemployment, sickness, or — as happened in at least three of the Asian households — when the man was also supporting a girlfriend and her children:

> One day, we lost the house because I was not able to pay the mortgage, and soon after that, he lost his ten year job because he was sick and not in for a long time. When these things happened, I was sad and so were my children. We had to move to a bed and breakfast place. (33)

> My husband has a house where he lives with his girl friend, and I am living with my children in my father-in-law's house. This house is in very poor condition and needs a lot of repairing which my husband never realised. (38)

In some cases, where the man is claiming benefit for the whole family but keeping it all for himself, it has been possible for the woman to claim her share of benefit separately for herself and her children. Most women were not aware of this possibility, however, until the intervention of a health visitor, social worker or other agency. Other women, who had left their husbands, or wished to do so, were not aware that they would then be able to claim Income Support in their own right. Parita Trivedi has argued that:

> Very few Asian women have the necessary resources to contemplate life on their own with anything but trepidation. With employment prospects grim, and welfare benefits inadequate, it is above all a fear of economic insecurity which drives women back to the marital home, and not cultural traditions. (Trivedi, 1984, p.49)

This should not, of course, be a surprise; it is also the situation of many white women who feel unable to support themselves and their children, and are forced to go back to their husbands because of poverty or financial insecurity. This situation is a symptom of the generally disadvantaged position of all women, and which, in the case of black women, is intensified by the racism as well as sexism which they face in British society.

Isolation

These practical difficulties can be exacerbated by the extreme isolation which many Asian women feel. Some Asian husbands are very reluctant to allow their wives to go out and make friends, even with other Asian women, and women who would like to attend language classes, for example, are sometimes forbidden to attend. Attitudes within certain sections of Asian communities and the relative scarcity of Asian support networks compound these problems, and women who have left their relatives in their home country experience this particularly strongly. Many Asian women have no idea where to go or whom to turn to if their partners begin to abuse them.

> I didn't have my own relatives in this country who could help me. I was isolated. Many times I decided to leave home but I couldn't because I didn't know where to go. (34)
> I told him, there is no way he can send us to Pakistan, and now he is saying that I should leave his house. I haven't got any relatives in this country, so where should I go? (49)
> I am depressed, I don't know what to do. (40)

It is important to recognise how central the family is in Asian communities in providing individuals with a feeling of belonging and as a means of support and advice. Women can gain a great deal of support from their extended family. This changes when a woman marries, as she would then normally live with her partner's family, who will treat her in a variety of ways reflecting their attitudes towards women, their position within the household, and the obligations of their sons, and, as we have said (p.), many women have no relatives of their own in this country.

> I used to live with my in-laws. It was very strange for me because my husband most of the time stayed out, sometimes three days at a time. (39)
> My husband doesn't feel any shame about (his adultery). His relatives try to make him understand but he doesn't care for anyone except her. Many times he has tried to bring her home, but I don't let him, and his brother said to me, they will support me in this. (48)
> When my husband said that he didn't want to live with the family, I said I couldn't do that. I needed to think about it... My mother-in-law is handicapped and I look after her. Sometimes she is OK with me, sometimes she is not. I have to do all the housework for all the family. One time I had trouble with my sister-in-law and my brother-in-law. It

82

got worse every day. My brother-in-law was violent to me and nobody supported me in the house. I had cuts and bruises. (34)

The relationship between a woman's in-laws and her children is often very important, and some women are reluctant to make any move which might jeopardise this relationship, or break up close ties based on affection and family feeling.

My son is very close to my mother-in-law and the family is good with my son, and that is enough for me. (34)

Sometimes families will condone or uphold their son's behaviour, as separation can reflect on the honour of the whole family:

My in-laws found me and I didn't have any choice, so I went back. (34)

Women themselves also felt under pressure to be a "good wife" and were very vulnerable to suggestions that their difficulties were of their own making, and that they should return home and try again. This is not, of course, exclusive to Asian women: many of the white women in our study were persuaded against their own interests and better judgement to go back to their abusive partners. But the particular isolation of some Asian women, many of whom had no alternative sources of support, made them especially susceptible to such pressure.

The woman's family

When a woman has the support of her family and is able to see them frequently, the difference is quite marked. Contrary to the usual perceptions many white people hold of Asian families, most of the women in our interviews were not ostracised by their own relatives if they decided to separate from their husbands, and the sympathy and help they received was often much appreciated.

My brother-in-law and my sister said to him that he should leave the house. There was no relationship left between him and me, and they said I was not going back to him. They have been very good to me. (46)
I said to my parents, I am going for divorce. My parents weren't able to say anything because it was very sad for them because they arranged the marriage. They didn't think my marriage was going to end that soon... I have now got my parents here and they are happy too. (39)

Another woman returned for a while to her parents in Pakistan:

My parents were helping me. They said to me, you shouldn't go back to him, because he is no good. He hasn't got any feeling for his children and me. (33)

Sometimes a woman's family will try to reconcile the couple, but not to the extent that they will over-ride the woman's feelings or condone the man's violent or adulterous behaviour:

My auntie and uncle are trying to change him, but I don't want him now. (33)

In contrast, a woman's isolation is exacerbated if her relatives are not in this country and she cannot manage to see them:

> I haven't seen my parents for seven years. They wanted to see me and I wanted to see them but it's very difficult for me to go because I need quite a lot of money... I hope to see my parents soon, and when I go, they will decide for my future, and it's very important to me to have my parents' advice. (34)
>
> I have been through court for divorce and custody and an injunction. It was a very hard time for me because I didn't have my closest relatives in this country. I have an auntie in England, but at that time, she used to live in a different city. (33)

Although many Asian women received considerable support from their families, this was not without its own attendant problems. Women were often criticised by the wider community if they made positive moves to leave their violent husbands, and the repercussions could extend to their families (both older and younger generations) making it a much harder step to take. Asian women sometimes met with disapproval and even ostracism rather than respect and support. A woman who is experiencing doubt or misgivings about approaching the law for protection may have these feelings reinforced by her awareness of her community's attitude towards marriage, separation, and the involvement of solicitors and the courts.

> Our community will look down on me if I have a divorce from this husband. I won't be able to get help from the community. They tend to blame the woman rather than the man. (33)
>
> I don't believe going to court would help. I think it would cause more problems. The Asian community doesn't like women going to court. The main thing is that a woman should get support from the community, that's the way the problems could be solved, but a woman who hasn't got parents in this country hasn't got that support. (34)

Concern for other members of their families also caused women to reconsider their initial decision to go for separation or divorce:

> Anyway, if I have a divorce, I am not going to get married again, so there is no point in me having a divorce, and I don't feel good about going to court because in India, women will not go to court whatever happens. It gives a bad name to a woman who goes to court, and I still feel the same. In this country anyway, a court can only help with divorce or separation, and that I don't want. (48)
>
> I will find it hard to arrange marriages for my children, the community will not see us as a good family because their father has a bad name. (48)

It is important, however, to note that, as in the last quote, it is the man's behaviour — in this case, both violent abuse and adultery — which is being condemned as much as or more than that of his wife.

While his actions may reflect on his wife and their children, it is clear that it is he and not she who is being held responsible. Domestic violence is no more acceptable in Asian families than it is in white European ones, but the motives to keep quiet and to try to deal with it in their own way may be particularly strong. The men, too, often feel the need to respond to this moral pressure:

> My husband didn't like the idea of getting a divorce. He wanted to come back and live with us because he cares about us and he doesn't want the community to talk about him and his family. (38)

Nevertheless, in spite of these difficulties and pressures, some Asian women did persist in obtaining effective protection for themselves and their children.

Courts and other agencies

Some Asian women do approach a solicitor and go to court, though probably in much smaller proportions than in the white English community. Again, language is an obstacle to a woman's access to information and services, and opinions as to their usefulness are mixed. Often the approach of an individual solicitor may be the most important factor, but even so there are many emotional and cultural barriers standing in the way of Asian women seeking legal protection. Moreover, the repercussions in terms of the attitude of the community may increase her sense of isolation, and there is a general lack of understanding by agencies who are not equipped to deal with the needs of Asian women.

> The next day, I went to a solicitor with my friend and I told him everything. I had an injunction out against him... When he saw me coming home, he was very angry but he didn't hit me. Next day he was OK. I was quite happy. I thought he had learnt his lesson — but it didn't last long. (46)
> I went to the solicitor and a court and had a divorce. I do feel that the solicitor and the court were helpful to me. I speak little English, that was a problem, but my friend who is a relative to me as well, she was very helpful to me. (39)

The fairly rigid structure of the law and the courts are often not appropriate to Asian women. Many of the women we interviewed approached other agencies for help. Some of these approaches were successful, but some not. Social workers can sometimes help, if women have been able to express their demands and have them met to some degree:

> I have a social worker. She is good. My health visitor arranged for it. I speak very little English, but my social worker always brings someone with her, to help communicate. (48)

I don't want to see a solicitor yet. I want the social worker to see my husband and warn him before I start to do anything against him. A male social worker might be better. (49)

The next day, he brought some close friends to the house, and my social worker (was there))and he said in front of them all that he would never (again) treat me the way he had been doing, and if he did, I could do what I liked... If I hadn't left home and seen the solicitor and the social worker, I believe I would have had to suffer for ever. (47)

Asian women — like women generally — often felt quite strongly that they wanted to see a female social worker; whereas they believed that their husbands would take notice only of a man. They would also often have preferred an Asian worker, who, they felt, could understand their situation fully, and treat it appropriately and sensitively. This was, however, often difficult or impossible to achieve; (see quote above, p79).

Another important source of support is Women's Aid, and its refuges. However, such refuges are often over-crowded and under-resourced, on the outskirts of cities and away from any community support network. They are often unable to make any special provision for Asian women — or, in fact, for black women generally. Workers and other women in the house may be ignorant of a woman's culture and needs, and sometimes she will experience outright racism, which will add enormously to her sense of isolation, and reinforce her doubts about her actions.

I went to a woman's refuge. I was the only Asian woman there. I didn't like the place. I wasn't able to do my Asian shopping for food... I didn't get any help from them because of my language problems. (34)

My friend left home once, and she came back because the woman's refuge wasn't any good for her. She didn't like it. Now her husband is treating her even worse. (49)

After that, I had to go into a women's refuge. I found it very difficult, with the language and other problems. (46)

All but two of the Asian women in our sample either found living in a refuge intolerable to them, or they said very firmly that they would not consider it, because such refuges were suitable for white women only. An article[4] written by black women who work for an Asian Resource Centre in Brent points out that:

The last thing a woman wants when she seeks shelter in a refuge is to have her cultural traditions and values attacked by women who feel they know and understand what is best for her. The experience of being subjected to violence by men, although uniting women, can also form the basis for racist assumptions and stereotyping about men in general and black men in particular. (p.85, *ibid.*)

It is for reasons like this that women in some cities have established refuges purely for black women, (many of these specifically for Asian women), staffed by black workers[5]. WAFE's policy is to encourage the development of such refuges, and, wherever possible, to offer black women the choice of a black refuge, if they wish. At present, however, in many areas of the country, women do not have such a choice. It is in any case extremely important that workers and volunteers in all refuges work hard not only to understand the particular needs of black women, but to challenge and eradicate their own racist attitudes and practices, and those of the residents, so that we can move towards a situation in which refuges can become safe and welcoming environments for *all* women.

Conclusion

Both black and white women experience similar problems in trying to get effective protection from violent men. For black women, however, these problems are exacerbated by racism, by cultural and language differences, by isolation, and, often, by poverty, bad housing and unemployment which are more widespread among the black population. Moreover, some women, who have recently come to Britain, perhaps on marriage, or to accompany a husband who is a student or has a temporary contract, may find that — at least initially — their residential status is dependent on that of their husbands. If they leave home, they may be at risk of deportation; and in any case, they may not have "recourse to public funds" — which means, for example, that they cannot claim Income Support or accommodation under the homelessness legislation (*Alibhai*, 1989).

As part of our overall recommendations which we make in our concluding chapter, we would like to make a number of recommendations specifically aimed at improving the position of black women. Firstly, an interpreting service should be established in all cities, for the use of individual solicitors and courts. Its existence should be widely publicised, and it should be available, and paid by legal aid, for anyone who needs it. Secondly, adequate funding should be made available to groups wishing to set up refuges or advice centres specifically for black women. Clearly, these refuges should be staffed by black women and should have adequate specialist advice services on which they could call as necessary. Thirdly, immigration law should be reviewed so that a woman's status is never dependent on that of a man; and the rule by which, for the first year of marriage, a woman's residential status is conditional on the relationship continuing should be abolished. Finally, all statutory and voluntary agencies should review their policies and practices with the aim of eliminating racism. Of particular importance in this connection is the recruitment of black workers to key positions — as homelessness officers, social workers, police officers, lawyers, magistrates and the judiciary. Just as a woman may often prefer to turn to a female professional to give her support and advice regarding domestic violence and other sensitive issues, so too may many black women find it much easier to talk to another black woman, and feel that they receive greater understanding and more appropriate support from her. The freedom to make this choice should be available to any woman.

Footnotes

1. Many of the case studies detailed in this book show how women often felt morally obligated to offer to share their accommodation with boy friends who arrived homeless on their doorsteps. (Mama, 1989)
2. Although numbers are small, it is important to note that these eleven women constitute one third of the total sample interviewed for this study.
3. Amina Mama, however, stresses that other black women, who may *not* be financially dependent, but in contrast are perhaps the main breadwinners in their households, are nonetheless not immune from domestic violence (*op. cit.* pp. 88 and 122.)
4. "Black women organising autonomously" *Feminist Review*17 (1984) (pp.83-99). See also Parmar (1982); Guru (1986).
5. See Mama (1989, pp.290-293) and Guru (1986) for a full discussion of these issues.

CHAPTER 6:
THE VIEWS OF THE PROFESSIONALS.

Although this study has been undertaken primarily from the point of view of the women who are themselves experiencing violence, we feel that the viewpoint of some of the professional workers involved can be helpful in complementing this perspective and in illuminating some of the problems women face. This is particularly so in the case of Cumbria, where we were able to talk to very few women and witnessed very few court cases.

We are using the term "professional" to apply to anyone who, in the course of his or her work, is regularly called upon to help, advise or support women who are experiencing domestic violence. "Work" can, in this context, include paid employment (for example, a police officer, social worker or paid worker in a Women's Aid refuge), self employment (for example, many solicitors), or voluntary work (such as that undertaken by many who work for Citizens' Advice Bureaux or Women's Aid refuges.) In this study, the major "professional" group we talked to consisted of solicitors (four in Bristol, six in Kendal and other parts of Cumbria). In Cumbria, we also talked to one serving police officer, one retired police officer, one CAB volunteer, one paid refuge worker, three social workers, one magistrates' court clerk, one magistrate, one probation officer and the co-ordinator of a Victim Support group. We have also had informal communications with three judges and one barrister, all but one of whom were based in the Bristol area. As before, we will be focusing on the legal process, and we will be using our interviews with solicitors as a framework, while drawing on other material as appropriate.

Choosing a solicitor

Solicitors are often the first port of call for a woman who has decided to try to do something about a violent relationship. If she has never consulted a solicitor before, however, she may have difficulty in deciding which firm of solicitors to go to. There are a number of factors to consider: does the firm do legal aid work? is there a solicitor who specialises in matrimonial work? is s/he experienced in the procedures for obtaining emergency protection? does s/he have time to take on a new client immediately? does the solicitor seem sympathetic and understanding, and does s/he allow the woman sufficient time to talk fully about the things which are worrying her? Some of these questions can be answered quite simply by a representative of the firm or by an outside body such as CAB. Others are much harder, and often it is only after having used a certain solicitor for a time that a client may discover that perhaps he or she was not the right or the best person for the job.

Some women go initially to a CAB, to social services or (where available) to a Women's Centre or Women's Aid office, and may be referred on to a solicitor from there. The CAB is not able to recommend particular firms, but will pass on the names of one or more practices which do matrimonial work and offer legal aid. In Kendal, the CAB has a list of firms which are willing to take referrals from them, and their policy is to refer women to particular solicitors on a rota basis. This system is only by-passed if the woman's partner is known to use the firm in question. Social services have no official policy, but individual social workers may mention an individual solicitor if they are asked. Women's Aid groups and Women's Centres often maintain lists of solicitors they know are good (i.e. effective and sympathetic) in coping with domestic violence cases, and they may offer to accompany a woman on her first visit to a solicitor. Many of the solicitors they recommend will be women, who may often have a better understanding of the problems and feelings the woman is experiencing.

The particular difficulties in finding a solicitor may be different in urban and rural areas. In a city, the woman is faced with an enormous choice, often with very little guidance as to which firm may be best for her particular problem. Some of the smaller firms specialise in particular kinds of work, whereas within firms of all sizes, individual solicitors are likely to specialise. Many practices are extremely busy, and may be booked up for weeks ahead, which means they may have difficulty in taking on a lot of emergency work. Some firms limit their injunction work to existing clients. Others follow the practice of referring enquirers on to other firms if they do not have the space to see a woman the same day or the next day. One of the Bristol solicitors who was particularly sympathetic to this kind of problem explained:

> I try to see her as early as I can. I just judge how they sound on the 'phone. I speak to them myself and ask them if they feel they are in immediate danger, and if they have anywhere to go, and if they sound very distressed, then I usually get them to come in and I make a space for them on the day if I can. If I can't, and they really want to see somebody (straight away) then I suggest they go and see someone else, and I try to think of someone sympathetic and geographically feasible. (Solr 4, female, Bristol)

In rural areas, in contrast, it is very unlikely that the woman will be able to find a solicitor who has considerable experience of making injunction or personal protection applications. This may mean that the service she receives may not be as good as it should be. As one solicitor said to us:

> I have maybe two applications a year on the domestic side... I deal with it very badly, I think... I don't spend as much time as I should on matrimonial matters. I think most solicitors in general practice rather than specialising would probably say the same thing, if they were honest. (Solr 8, male, Cumbria)

On the other hand, most of the Cumbria solicitors felt they could almost always find time to see somebody, either immediately or later the same day, and certainly within twenty-four hours. They therefore did not have to refer women to other firms, and could often build up a personal relationship with their clients, who could ring them up at home if they needed them urgently.

> I have appointments throughout the day, but being a local area, people tend to pop in and say, "I want to see a solicitor"... Generally I would see people straight away. Certainly within twenty-four hours, and if somebody rang up and said it was urgent, unless I happened to be going to court with somebody, I would see them within the day. (Solr 8, male, Cumbria)
>
> Everybody knows where we live... Our numbers are in the phone book. (Solr 7, male, Cumbria)

Whether the advantage of this kind of personal service outweighs the lack of specialised knowledge is difficult to say. There is also an associated drawback, in that the solicitors may also have strong professional and personal links with some of the male abusers. This may mean they are reluctant to take on a case, or may even disbelieve a woman's story. Certainly it seems that clients in rural areas may have a very restricted choice — for example, women who would prefer a female solicitor may be unable to find one — and whereas the one available solicitor in the town or village may suit a particular woman very well, if this is not the case, then she may not have the option to go elsewhere. Moreover, if certain proposed changes to the legal aid system are put into effect, many small firms may be unable to offer legal aid, and this will, of course, have a drastic effect on the availability of legal advice to women in rural areas.

The first appointment with a solicitor

As we have stressed before, for a woman to consult a solicitor about a violent partner is an enormous step, and she will often feel hesitant, frightened and unhappy, and will need considerable reassurance and patience, if she is to tell her story in full, and be able to make wise choices about the next steps she will take. How solicitors handle this first interview is therefore of crucial importance.

As we have seen, the important elements, from the woman's point of view, are: being given ample time to explain their situation; a full explanation from the solicitor of the various options available; and being encouraged to say what they want to do. For many women, too, the solicitor's manner is as important, or more important, than these more practical issues: a solicitor who seems sympathetic, reassuring and unhurried, who treats the client with respect, and who inspires confidence that her problems can be solved, is very much valued. These more intangible factors are often harder to judge than professional competence or good practice.

Seven solicitors said, with various degrees of emphasis, that they always allowed a woman time to talk, and then explained in some detail the various options open to her.

> I try to explain the limits of what I can do for them, which can be very limited... It does take quite a long time to let someone tell their story in their own mind... It's difficult for us at this end to know how much information to give. I think I try to ask people what they want and what they think they're going to get and then I try to say what we can and cannot do, but it is very confusing; and it's also difficult when you're being bombarded with a lot of information from somebody who's in an emotional state and feeling very frightened, to take that on, and to respond sympathetically and constructively and get your own mind clear about what exactly you can do. (Solr 4, female, Bristol)

> Although we're obviously here to give legal advice, there are often other factors that are more important to the woman... e.g. will an injunction be effective? And at the end of the day, you've got to give as much information as you can to enable them to make a decision, though they're not always in a fit state to make that decision in the circumstances, and you sometimes have to give them a little push in the right direction. I try to give them the options and my advice as to which option to take, but in the end, it's their decision (Solr 2, male, Bristol)

> I think we do try to explain, we go through it all rather carefully, but I suppose if she's in a state, she may appear to take it in and understand what you say, but when she comes back next time, it's obvious that she hasn't. (Solr 9, male, Cumbria)

The amount of time solicitors thought it was appropriate to offer clients on a first interview often varied. Several solicitors said, or implied, that they would give up the best part of a day to an emergency injunction application. Some of the time would be spent reassuring the woman and listening to her, and the rest would be ensuring that the necessary affidavits and application forms were filled in with the utmost speed, and taken to court the same day. Other solicitors seemed to feel they could deal with the issue at least initially in a much shorter space of time.

> In theory, the kind of information you want you can get out of her in a quarter of an hour, no problem at all, because you recognise half the problem. "Has he done this? Has he done that?" and you know what happened from past experience. So it depends on the woman. You can be with her an hour, you can be with her a quarter of an hour. It just depends on each one. (Solr 6, male, Cumbria)

> I fix my appointments half an hour apart so that they get an automatic thirty minutes unless there is something else going on, and I can't spare the time on them. I'll always find time to see anybody who comes in, because running a matrimonial practice, you can't not do that, because they need reassurance there and then. If I needed to take a longer statement, I'd ask for it to be fixed in my diary for about an hour or an hour and a half... I get a good volume of clients in here who are quite happy with that system. Occasionally you feel sometimes that you don't do them justice, they want to talk to you for longer and you can't spare the time to do that. (Solr 5, male, Cumbria)

One solicitor said that it was not her job to reassure, or to act as a counsellor for her clients, but that she would refer women to other agencies (including Women's Aid) if she felt they could benefit from that kind of support. Another solicitor said that he only rarely had clients coming in a distraught state, and that most of the people he saw knew exactly what they wanted, and only needed him to ensure that they got it. Another solicitor said he tended to be abrupt and confident, and felt that this was the best way to assure the woman that her problems could be solved. In contrast to this approach, three solicitors said that they felt it was important to give their clients time to consider various options, and they liked to be sure that what was eventually decided upon was genuinely the woman's own choice.

Professionals' perceptions of clients.

How solicitors and other professionals respond to their clients will often depend on their general attitude to women and to domestic violence, and the views they hold about the people who consult them. It was clear that several solicitors held rather patronising views about their female clients:

> If you've got someone coming in who's upset, what can you do? "Right, love, we're going to do this" and you do it. If it's someone who comes in and wants to know what the options are, you explain it to them. The majority come in, "My husband is hitting me, I want it stopping". "Right, dear, this is what we can do to get it stopped for you". It depends on each one, really. (Solr 6, male, Cumbria.)

> Statistically speaking, one's clients tend to be at the working class end of the spectrum, where a belt around the head takes the place of reasoned

argument. (Solr 1, male, Bristol)

How far you go is certainly covered by what sort of level of personality and intelligence they have... Now if you've got a lady of very limited education, then you explain to her that yes, she can have a divorce, what the alternatives are on the facts as she's given them to you... Now a lady of different educational standing, you're going to explain the process to her, you're going to explain the rights and obligations of the partners, and the various options that may come forward and so on. (But otherwise) simply because they're a) distressed and b) they're of limited educational attainment, if you give a lot of technical stuff, then they just can't take it. (Solr 7B, male, Cumbria)

Although we only spoke to two female solicitors (and none in Cumbria) we feel it may be significant that neither of them spoke in such terms. Both of them seemed very conscious that *any* woman (including themselves) might one day be in a very similar situation to that of their clients. They did not make sweeping judgements in terms of class or supposed "intelligence", and nor did they limit their advice or their actions according to prejudiced perceptions of what they thought their clients might want.

These kinds of perceptions were sometimes shared by some of the other professional workers we spoke to:

If it was merely, "He's hit me with his fist in my face and I think he's broken my nose" that's normal domestic type of violence... (Maybe) the wife has had a few drinks herself, and there are varying types of wives... Sometimes you go into the room and find the wife there but nothing wrong with her, just a bit of blood, just a burst nose.... (Retired police officer, now with a voluntary agency)

(Interviewer: What advice would you give a woman who came to you and said she was being beaten up and what could she do?) CAB worker: Depends very much what sort of woman she is, and whether she is accompanied by anyone.... You're dealing basically with this sort of case, more with working class people than you are with middle class people who wouldn't probably gravitate automatically to a battered wives' home. (CAB volunteer)

These views were not held universally. Nevertheless, it is important to point out that these views run counter to all available research evidence, including our own, and a programme of re-education seems necessary, in rural areas particularly.

One difficulty that solicitors — even sympathetic ones — mentioned was the frustration they experienced when, having spent considerable time with a woman, including, perhaps, going to court with her, they then discovered that she had gone back home or allowed the man to return. Moreover, if these temporary "reconciliations" occurred on several occasions, and then the woman returned to the solicitor for further action, they sometimes felt very dissatisfied that she was unable

94

to see the procedure through:

> There is a lot of widespread frustration among solicitors about doing this kind of work. Everything gets pushed to one side, you're running round like hell trying to get this straight, and quite often the women don't follow it through. They come to court, and next week they say they're not really interested, and I can understand why they're not really interested, but it does tend to create that picture, a sort of myth of "Oh those women!" which is fairly pervasive. (Solr 4, female, Bristol)

> I must say there is some cursing goes on between me and my secretary, "Mrs. Bloggs has come in again", but having said that, they don't get treated any differently. (Solr 5, male, Cumbria)

Among solicitors practising in rural areas, there seemed to be a common belief that violence was relatively rare, and that most cases could be fairly easily settled by the woman going to her mother's for a few days or weeks, either until things calmed down, or an amicable separation could be arranged. This view also seemed to be shared by many of the other professionals working in Cumbria. The following comment was typical of many:

> As a rural area, it is still a very close-knit community, still slightly the nuclear family... (One woman) came to me on Monday morning, and she was badly bruised and I could see the bruising, she had two children, eleven and eight, and her husband had thrown her out the night before, so she went to her parents. You see, they would go to their parents, or an aunt or uncle, in this sort of area. (CAB volunteer)

Whether or not such optimism was borne out by the reality we have no way of knowing. What is clear, however, is that women who do need to escape from a persistently violent man will find this much harder in an area like Kendal, where (as we were told) "everybody knows everybody", and the chances of re-housing either in or outside the area seem to be very slight. The social workers we spoke to in Kendal seemed to be the only professionals who were really aware of this as a potential problem:

> Rural areas have poor support networks in some ways. A lot of their support networks are excellent but they're family-based. (Social worker 1)

> The council has now re-opened the Homeless Families hostel and they would concede accommodating someone temporarily if she was a victim of domestic violence. They would regard her as temporarily homeless but they would insist that she try to get possession of the matrimonial home... They would say there is a legal remedy and she must take it. (Social worker 2)

Unfortunately we did not have the opportunity to talk to anyone from the Housing Department to check on what their policy was, but if it is as reported to us, it seems to be in contravention of the homelessness legislation (see Chapter 2, p23). It was also pointed out to us that even if a woman were to be re-housed, the only council estate on which she could be placed was very well known, and it would be easy enough to trace anyone who was living there. In Bristol and other large cities, it may be easier to get alternative accommodation well away from where the ex-partner is living. We return to this point below (p117).

Legal Aid

If a solicitor is to provide any more than a short initial interview (which may be covered under the Green Form Scheme) either the client must have sufficient funds to cover the often very substantial costs, or legal aid must be applied for. In the normal way, this takes from six to eight weeks, but in an emergency, it may be obtained much more rapidly, sometimes agreement being obtained over the 'phone straight away.

Solicitors vary both in their willingness to apply for emergency legal aid (over the telephone or otherwise) and in their ability to obtain it. One solicitor said that emergency legal aid was only available for very serious injuries, and another said that he would only apply for it very occasionally, as otherwise he would be "debasing the coinage" and perhaps find it harder to get when, in his view, it was "really necessary". Others mentioned other limitations; for example, that legal aid was not available for an injunction when there had been only one violent incident; and that it was much harder to obtain when the parties did not live together, or when there had been several previous applications; or that they had been asked to go to the magistrates' court for a personal protection order (which can be obtained under ABWOR[1], and is therefore much cheaper) rather than applying to the county court for an injunction. Two solicitors were of the view that legal aid was now harder to get than it used to be:

> Perhaps we lawyers tend to put on the legal aid fund many more cases than we might have done say five years ago, ten years ago, and therefore the Legal Aid Board is somewhat more sceptical about granting legal aid for work like that unless there are really substantial grounds. (Solr 7B, male, Cumbria)
>
> The main problem is how quickly you can get your legal aid. There is no doubt about it, you have to wait longer than you did say five years ago, and it becomes even more difficult if the woman has made applications for legal aid injunctions previously. I think the Legal Aid Board are becoming tougher. (Solr 2, male, Bristol)

One solicitor believed strongly that the Legal Aid Board were "capricious" in their decisons regarding legal aid applications:

I tried to get legal aid for a free-standing injunction in September last year and it was refused. (Interviewer: Why?) Who knows? They give reasons but the reasons are so vague: "It's not considered reasonable to expend public money on these proceedings". That could mean anything, it just means "No", it's just a long way of saying it. In that particular case, I suspect the reason was that they thought there wasn't any serious violence involved, which happened to be the case. However, in January this year, I had another case which was virtually on all fours with it, from a fact point of view, and I got legal aid just like that!... According to your client's surname, you get a frosty or a reasonably pleasant reception. (Solr 1, male, Bristol)

Those solicitors who in contrast had few or no problems with legal aid put it down to their being known and trusted by the people working in their local legal aid office:

I can be on the 'phone to the Law Society (sic) ... speak to any one of half a dozen executive officers. They know me, know I would honour an undertaking to send off the signed forms that day, and they know I wouldn't be applying for emergency legal aid unless it *was* an emergency. (Solr 5, male, Cumbria)

You can't always persuade them on the phone that it's needed there and then on the day. I think fortunately we know them down at the legal aid office reasonably well, and they know that when we say, "Look, this really is an ex parte injunction," they normally will accept that. (Solr 2, male, Bristol)

In a sense, such comments bear out the criticism that the legal aid authorities are "capricious". Rather than being decided merely on the merits of the woman's case, it seems that the (supposed) merits of the *solicitor* will be taken into account as well. Moreover, since applications are allocated to legal aid officers on the basis of the clients' surnames, some clients may be disadvantaged from the start because the officer dealing with their case takes a harder line than the others, or feels less favourable to the solicitor making the application.

Procedure for applying for a court order

Several solicitors, particularly in Bristol, were very conscious of the time that injunction work took up. Apart from the initial reassurance and listening to the woman's story, there was the time taken in typing affidavits (if the case was to be taken to the county court) and filling out the necessary court forms (as well as the legal aid application forms, which had to be completed immediately, even if legal aid had been agreed, in principle, over the telephone). Some solicitors tried to get the case into court the same day, and this could involve some waiting around while a space could be found. One solicitor gave in detail an example of an emergency injunction application that he had dealt with the previous week:

They arrived about 9. Now we had the injunction served by the evening, but we were 9 to 12.30 drafting the affidavit here. That meant she told me the story and I was writing it up, getting it typed, all the way along, so we were a page or two behind. We then had to go across to the court and issue just before lunch, and that means then that you've got to find when you have a judge free, and normally that is straight after lunch, 2.15. Got the injunction ex parte by 2.30, and then of course the orders have to be engrossed and issued also, that's got to be sealed by the court, that took another hour or so. I had a draft order actually in my sticky paw but the judge wanted a little bit of modification to it, and I didn't want just to have a hand written amended order, so that had to be typed out, that went back for sealing, then I got my process servers in. We've got a very good firm, come and collect from the premises, and they took it out and it was served by 6 or 7 o'clock, but that's most of the day. And because of the nature of the application, you can't use court messengers to do the donkey work, to take it across to court and get it issued, and that's because you've got to know what you're doing. And it's slightly outside normal procedure where they like to take the papers and issue them, and you're saying, "I want it now". You've got to know how to do it, and in fact it involved me personally all day. (Solr 1, male, Bristol)

Another solicitor pointed out that:

It's sometimes a problem to drop everything else, and I'm well aware that if it's an emergency, and sometimes my other work has been put back and put back and put back, and although it wasn't an emergency then, it's getting urgent and I'm having to deal with the pressure and stress of saying yes to one client and no to ten others in effect. (Solr 3, female, Bristol)

For those solicitors who use the magistrates' court the procedure was rather simpler since there was no requirement to have a detailed affidavit, and, in some areas, the magistrates were very accessible and could see a client and her solicitor straight away:

I think the (procedure) for magistrates' court is about as simple as you can get without going too far the other way... You've got a situation now where they can get an order without anything being served on the husband. You can't get anything much easier than that. (Solr 6, male, Cumbria)

Solicitors were divided as to whether the application procedure could be simplified. Some felt that there was very little that could be done, if both sides were to have a fair hearing. Many of them preferred having written affidavits whether they were acting for the applicant or the respondent, as they felt it made the whole thing much clearer and more straightforward for both the clients and themselves. (See below, "Choice of Courts"). Others felt that it would be much easier if the legislation was rationalised, so that both the criteria for obtaining an order and the application procedures were the same for all courts, whatever legislation was used, and whether or not the parties were married, cohabiting, or had not lived together at all.

> It would be better, I think, if we had less diverse options. If we could have — for instance, we have a bunch of lay magistrates, we have a legally qualified registrar, we've got two judges who do some of these things... I think it would be easier... if there was one court with all the powers which could adopt a conciliatory approach if that was needed or an adversarial approach if there was a dispute. (Solr 5, male, Cumbria)

> The actual jurisdiction could be rationalised, I'm sure. You could have a standard application covering all domestic situations. The main problem really at the moment is couples who aren't within the meaning of the jurisdiction (of the DVA) and then you're in the crazy position of having to take out trespass injunctions, and you can't get a power of arrest on that. (Solr 4, female, Bristol)

The difficulty of getting protection once divorce was made absolute, and the inability to get powers of arrest on a "trespass" injunction were also mentioned. We will present our own views on how the legislation could be improved in our concluding chapter.

Emergencies out of hours

One of the intentions of the existing legislation was that judges and magistrates should be available at *all* times to cope with grave emergencies which cannot wait until the next regular court. However, the first problem for a potential client is finding a solicitor who deals with civil work and who is available out of hours. (Criminal solicitors seem to be much more readily available, and the police station has contact numbers). This seems to be more of a problem in urban areas — where solicitors home numbers may be much harder to pick out of a telephone directory, and where they may in any case be less disposed to take on work out of hours except for an established and well known client. Many solicitors may in fact feel unable to be on regular call (for example if they have family or other commitments) though they are usually prepared to act for one of their existing clients, and in some cases, when they feel it is justified, they may then give them an out of hours contact number.

Even if the woman has got in contact with her solicitor, there is no guarantee that anything further can be done. Two solicitors said that they would find it difficult or impossible to get in touch with a judge out of hours — one of them saying that in fact she had no idea how to do so. Another solicitor felt that magistrates might be rather easier to get hold of (a fact that was confirmed by the magistrates' court clerk we spoke to — see below.)

> You try getting a judge at any time! That's easier said than done... There is a rota of judges but you've got to find them. The problem is not the judges, the problem is the court staff. There is supposed to be a duty court officer... You've got to get hold of him and he knows where the duty judge is, but it's in London. (Solr 1, male, Bristol)
> Easy to get hold of a magistrate but virtually impossible for us to get hold of a judge... If it was that serious that I had to do something at that time on a weekend, I think I would opt for a magistrate. (Solr 5, male, Cumbria)
> It's very very rare... but I have called out courts if need be at 10 o'clock, 10.30 at night... The police have the numbers of the three clerks and all communication should be through those numbers. We don't have a rota of who's on call because that's not practical, we're simply not called out that often... (Magistrates' Courts' Clerk)

Overall, however, the position of women needing protection out of hours seemed to be grim, and we believe more thought should be given to devising a system which is widely known, workable and effective. The police, as the only agency regularly and universally on call twenty-four hours a day, could keep a rota of solicitors prepared to be on call for emergency injunction work (and perhaps other domestic and civil matters, e.g. abduction of a child), and they could also keep contact numbers for magistrates and judges (or their clerks) so that an emergency court could be called very rapidly. We will return to this point in our concluding chapter.

Choice of court

In many cases, a woman may have the option of applying for a court order to protect her from a violent partner either in a magistrates' court or in a county court. In practice, this choice will almost always be made for her by her solicitor, who will take into consideration not only legal factors (such as which legislation applies best to each particular case; see Chapter 2) but the likelihood that the desired order will be granted, the relative costs, speed, local factors and personal preference.

Of the ten solicitors we spoke to, five said they preferred to use the county court, and almost invariably did so. Only one said that he would automatically use the magistrates' court, and he was one of three solicitors in Cumbria who pointed out that, in their area, the judge discouraged injunction applications.

Among the reasons for preferring the county court were: a preference for affidavit evidence over oral evidence used in the magistrates' court (four solicitors); knowing and trusting the judges (two solicitors); and the belief that an order made by a judge had greater power than one made by magistrates.

Certainly it has got about town, in my experience, that people will go to no end of lengths to get into the county court rather than the magistrates' court. The county court is an easier system to work somehow. I don't feel terribly happy doing domestic things in the magistrates' court at all... It's more formal, so there's proper paperwork to work from, you know what sort of case you've got to answer or what case you're putting forward. But in the magistrates' court, all you do is, you bang in a complaint and the allegations aren't specified. If you're acting for the respondent, you turn up in court having absolutely no idea what you're going to be faced with... It's not difficult to present a case properly but it's very difficult to defend a case when you've got no paperwork and don't know the substance of the allegations that are being made about you. (Solr 7B, male, Cumbria)

The judges just have... a much greater understanding and experience or these cases (than magistrates). They've been barristers themselves, usually, some of them have even been solicitors themselves, they know what these cases are about, they know what is being aimed for, they know how to read the affidavits and sort of pluck the verbiage from the actual facts, and I think they have more authority as well. I mean obviously they have more authority in terms of the judicial hierarchy, but I think they can be more intimidating to a man, I think they can actually impose more fear in a man. (Solr 3, female, Bristol)

Three solicitors said they distrusted magistrates, either because they were lay people and not legally trained, or because they could never know in advance which magistrates would be sitting on any particular day. Two said that in their experience, magistrates required a higher standard of proof and a greater level of violence than the county court judge. (This is to some extent borne out by our court records: none of the women applying for exclusion orders in the magistrates' court obtained them, though this sample is, of course, very small).

I don't have enough confidence in the magistrates' court. They don't do enough of them and they don't know what they're doing. OK, you may get it reasonably quickly and therefore cheaply, but you might have to be going back more times than you would for the county court. At least although the procedure is a bit long-winded in the county court, we do enough of it for it to run efficiently. (Solr 2, male, Bristol)

The problem you get in the magistrates' court as well is that they tend to require a standard of proof that they would require in a criminal case, and that's different from the standard of proof that you would require before a judge... You're far more likely to get an injunction from a judge than you are to get a protection order in the magistrates' court from the magistrates, because they don't approve of "reasonable doubt". (Solr 7, male, Cumbria)

In contrast, one solicitor felt that the magistrates were likely to be more sympathetic and grant the order more easily. Other reasons for preferring the magistrates' court included the fact that it was cheaper, there was less paperwork, and the magistrates were more accessible. Local practices seem very significant here. In Bristol, very few solicitors use the magistrates' court at all for this kind of case, and the county court judges seem to be very accessible and willing to fit in *ex parte* applications without delay. In Kendal, in contrast, there is a judge available only twice a month. This means that solicitors wishing to use the county court will usually have to travel to a town or city some way away. Moreover, the judge who most regularly sits in Kendal feels that most injunction applications should more properly be taken to the magistrates' court for personal protection orders instead:

> The judge prefers us to go to the magistrates' court and says that is what they are there for and should be used. (Solr 6, male, Cumbria)
> We do tend to have in this area judges who believes that domestic violence should be dealt with in the magistrates' court and are not very enthusiastic. (Solr 9, male, Cumbria)

In some other parts of Cumbria, the normal practice appears to be to go first before a Registrar who will consider the evidence and, if the man is also present, will expect in the first instance to be offered an undertaking. (The Registrar is not empowered to make orders).

> We have a system whereby the Registrar ... will hear applications. He can't actually make the orders... because he hasn't got the powers by the court to do it. All he can do is accept an undertaking from the respondent that he will leave within so many days, or he will not molest his wife or children or whatever... If the respondent... doesn't give an undertaking to the registrar... the Registrar takes offence because he likes to think he can get them all sorted out with undertakings, and he would then ensure that the judge heard it within a couple of days. (Solr 5, male, Cumbria)

This system of course cannot apply to *ex parte* orders, and has the effect that only in exceptional circumstances will a case be heard *ex parte* in areas where Registrars are often used for injunction cases.

The magistrate and the court clerk we interviewed were, naturally, and in contrast to many of the solicitors, very much in favour of using the forum of the magistrates' court for domestic violence and other related work. The court clerk pointed out that the "traditional answer" to the question of why the magistrates' court might be preferable was "in terms of speed", and that if an emergency matter was brought to his court, he would "pull out all the stops to do it." One study that compared the use of the magistrates' and county courts for a number of domestic matters where there was overlapping jurisdiction confirmed that, overall, the magistrates' courts*were* quicker in emergency cases (Murch *et al.*, 1987). However, in Avon, (which was one of the three areas included in the study) exceptionally, the county courts were marginally quicker than the magistrates' courts, hence endorsing, in this respect, the automatic preference of the Bristol solicitors in the current study.

Another advantage of using the magistrates, cited by the court clerk, was the fact that, as a lay tribunal, they might have a greater understanding of these kinds of situations than a legally qualified "professional judge". This, of course, is the reverse of what most of the solicitors believed.

The magistrate we spoke to confirmed what the clerk had said regarding speed. She said that they were trying all the time to improve their service, in consultation with solicitors, probation officers, and other users of the court system. She felt that the legislation gave magistrates the powers to provide effective protection to women, within a more informal and comfortable setting than that of the average county court.

Barristers

Another difference between Bristol and Cumbria was in the use of barristers. This is in some respects linked to the choice of court, since to use a barrister at a magistrates' court hearing was extremely unusual and would probably not be approved by the Legal Aid authorities. However, even when the county court procedure was preferred, solicitors in the rural area rarely if ever used barristers, whereas many (not all) solicitors in the city instructed counsel as a matter of course. Another reason for this difference was in the accessibility of barristers: in Bristol, there are a number of chambers of barristers, several of whom specialise in injunction work; in Kendal, barristers would have to come from Manchester or Liverpool, and this both increases the costs and makes it much less easy for the solicitor to instruct counsel beforehand.

The three solicitors (all in Bristol) who told us they would normally use barristers for injunction work, said that it saved their time, and was therefore cheaper for their firms, and that they had confidence in the skills of the barristers they instructed. One of them explained his reasons in some detail:

I always without exception use counsel for injunctions. It saves everybody's time. There are a couple of experts who pick up six injunctions in a morning. They get a single brief fee, so if they're there till 4 o'clock in the afternoon, they don't get paid any more. If I'm hanging around in court, from 10.30 till 4.30, I'm on an hourly rate and... it's all going to come off the client's money in the end, on the statutory charge[3], so I've got to think of their money and I've also got to think of saving my time... The barristers are very good at it. I leave them to it... (Two of them in particular) have the facility which I think is admirable of giving each client their total attention while they're talking to them, even though they have six or seven other cases in the same court. And they're very good hagglers... A lot of men turn up unrepresented and if you've got a good barrister, who doesn't adopt a condescending approach, he can often have quite a good conciliatory effect by simply saying to the chap, you know, isn't this something you should be thinking of, instead of just blustering? (Solr 1, male, Bristol)

Another Bristol solicitor (spoken to informally but not part of the interview sample), explained that the hourly rate that legal aid paid for "waiting time" at court was too low to make it worthwhile for a solicitor to spend time waiting with the woman. Instead, his firm gave this waiting work to an articled clerk, who would liaise between the client and the barrister. (The barrister is, technically, instructed by the solicitor and not directly by the client, and therefore a representative of the solicitor's firm must stay with the client all the time.)

Although it is apparently cheaper to use barristers where the waiting time is likely to be long, and when one barrister can do several injunction applications in one morning, in rural areas — where neither of these factors applies — it is apparently more profitable for the solicitor to go to court in person. As one solicitor explained:

Putting it bluntly, domestic violence injunctions, if you do them yourself, they're quite a good little earner, you know. You're not making a fortune out of it but they're all right. And if you use a barrister (you lose that). (Solr 7, male, Cumbria)

This solicitor seemed uninterested in whether or not his usual practice was in the best interests of his client. In contrast to this, two solicitors — who also customarily conducted injunction applications themselves — argued that this was to the advantage of the women, as barristers, however good they may be at advocacy, often lacked the personal touch:

I think there are a lot of firms who don't particularly care for injunction work who aren't that committed to the relationship with the women concerned, they quite often send barristers along, they have no emotional response with the clients. (Solr 3, female, Bristol)

Quite often, you've seen a client twice in the last week and they feel happy that you know what you've told them (sic), they may not feel happy if you bring in a barrister who has perhaps only picked up the papers before he gets on the train in the morning... He makes simple mistakes like calling one of the children by the wrong name or something, and the clients don't feel desperately happy about whether this chap is really representing them. (Solr 5, male, Cumbria)

In all, five solicitors said they would never use barristers for injunction or personal protection applications, four of these being in practice in Cumbria. One of these said he would instruct a barrister if a case came up for a committal hearing. Another Cumbria solicitor said that he would only use a barrister in "exceptional" cases, where perhaps the application was being strongly opposed, and the respondent was thought likely to instruct counsel. In Bristol, on the other hand, judging from our court observations, between half and three quarters of injunction applications in the county court are conducted by barristers, and there is anecdotal evidence that the proportion is increasing, partly because of changes in the rates of legal aid. There seems to be no evidence that applications made by barristers are either more or less likely to be successful, and whether or not this practice is to the advantage of clients is also uncertain.

Court facilities and procedures

There was general agreement among the solicitors we talked to that the facilities provided and the waiting areas at the courts were not at all good. Mostly, their complaints echoed those of the women we interviewed (see previous chapters) and our own experiences, but they generally said much less about this issue than the women themselves, indicating that it was rather less salient to them. In Bristol, the consensus of opinion was that matters had improved a lot recently, since, in order to alleviate over-crowding, injunctions cases had now mostly been moved to a separate court building, where there were two waiting rooms, one of which was set aside for women only. In Cumbria, the court buildings were generally very old, and often with no waiting facilities whatsoever. In Kendal, a new court building had been promised and planned for a number of years, but was now under construction and scheduled for completion within the next couple of years. In one of the other areas we visited (Whitehaven) a new court had recently been built and was very much appreciated by all who used it.

Among specific suggestions, solicitors mentioned the need for a creche or play facilities, for those women who had no alternative but to bring their young children with them to court; and some provision for refreshments. One solicitor pointed out that it was very difficult to get children's push-chairs into most court buildings — which tended to have steps up to the main door, and heavy doors which were awkward to open when pushing a child and perhaps looking after other children as well. This of course would be equally difficult for clients in wheel chairs. Although there was a lift inside all those courts in which upstairs rooms were used, in at least one case, this was small, old, and inconspicuous, and many members of the public might not be aware of its existence.

One solicitor was sensitive to the fact that the court waiting areas have a generally "clubby" atmosphere which can exclude those who do not really belong:

> I sometimes think that when you're in the courts regularly inevitably you know all the people there and there can be... a bit of a clubby atmosphere. You know, people come in, "Hello, Jim." "Hello." It's nobody's fault, it's just nature. (Solr 8, male, Cumbria)

Another woman took a rather different angle when she suggested that some women could find the presence of other women, all going through the same thing, very supportive and encouraging:

> They do have a women-only waiting room where women can spend some time getting to know each other. I think that can be quite supportive. I think it's very important for women to realise, particularly women who either don't know of Women's Aid or don't want to be in touch at all... that they do learn to realise that there are women maybe from different classes, different backgrounds, different racial origins, all experiencing the same problem. That can be quite supportive. (Solr 3, female, Bristol)

This situation is, of course, much more likely to be present in urban courts than in rural ones, when the shared interests and camaraderie of the lawyers will still apply, but the clients are likely to be there for many different reasons.

In busy courts, where there are many injunction applications, as in Bristol, it is apparently impossible to list cases for particular times and stick to this closely. The need — from the point of view of the court staff — is to get all the cases heard as quickly and efficiently as possible. The convenience of the judge seems to be the first priority, and after that comes the wish to clear the waiting area as quickly as possible. Therefore, cases which are heard in open court (such as committals, when injunctions and undertakings have been breached) are heard first, followed by the most straightforward of the injunction applications, where no contest is expected.

> You never know before you get there which (cases) are going to be quick and which aren't. And the principle is, you get the list moving, get the fast ones out of the way, save any that are likely to be contested cases until you've got a lot of other stuff out of the way. And then you don't know how many judges are going to be available. What happens now, as far as I can make out, is that one judge is allocated... and if another judge gets free... they will take half of the rest of the list. They'll split it between them, but it is a juggling act which ushers are absolutely wonderful at doing, but I can't see any other way of doing it, except listing them all for the same time. (Solr 1, male, Bristol)

In the magistrates' courts, even in Bristol, it seems easier to keep to specific times, and this is also the case at all the courts in Kendal and other parts of Cumbria. Although we can understand the difficulties facing staff at very busy urban courts, we feel that if some way of overcoming the problem of excessive waiting time could be devised, it would be very much appreciated both by the clients and their legal representatives.

With regard to the court proceedings themselves, there was a general feeling that court rooms are almost inevitably intimidating, and that going to court is always going to be stressful whatever may be done to try to make people feel more comfortable about it. One solicitor went further than this to suggest that the stress came from the broken relationship and from the relative positions of the woman and the man within that relationship, rather than from the court appearance itself:

> I think the stress is terrible in the courts but maybe the reality is that the stress comes from the relationship and maybe we're talking about social conditions rather than the day in court everyone focuses on. (Solr 3, female, Bristol)

She, together with two other solicitors (and the magistrate) also suggested that the formality of the procedure might be necessary in order to convince the violent men that their actions were unacceptable, and would be taken seriously.

> I think it's hard for the woman, but I think it's quite useful for the men so I don't know how you get a better balance... I think the court has to be intimidating so that the men realise that it's serious, but equally, I think it's quite hard for women to come into. (Solr 3, female Bristol)
> A great deal of the benefit of the court hearing is to frighten the man with the formality so I don't think they should necessarily be in a more congenial setting... (but they) do need to be humanised. I think the pomp is very off-putting. (Solr 4, female, Bristol)

Three solicitors felt there were certain relatively minor things that could be changed, such as the "ridiculous" clothes that barristers and judges wear. (In fact, when in chambers, the wigs and sometimes the robes are usually abandoned.) An equal number of solicitors believed, however, either that it was not possible to make the proceedings any less formal than they already were (given the humanising changes that have been made in some courts recently), or that they *should* not be.

Obtaining court orders

The three main issues that we raised with solicitors regarding the orders which they obtained for their clients were the criteria for exclusion orders, and those for getting powers of arrest; and their use of undertakings. The first two issues resulted in very little discussion. On the whole, the solicitors we talked to felt there were no real

107

problems in obtaining either an exclusion order or the addition of powers of arrest to an order, when these were justifiable. One solicitor said that exclusion orders could never be automatic, and that they would not be granted if custody were disputed, until welfare reports had been obtained. (This was, however, denied by several other solicitors of whom we asked this question specifically, and one of the judges we approached informally also said that, if such a situation arose, and exclusion seemed justifiable or necessary for the woman's safety, he would be prepared to hold the interim custody hearing the same afternoon or the next day.) Another solicitor said that, in his opinion, it was right that exclusion orders should not be available *ex parte* (a view which seems to be held by many lawyers, who regard property rights as at least an equal consideration to physical safety.)

Only two solicitors talked at any length about the availability of powers of arrest. This lack of comment seems to indicate that most solicitors believe there is no real issue, since an order by itself should, in most cases, be sufficient protection. One solicitor thought that the whole procedure for powers of arrest was extremely demanding on the court staff and the police, and that perhaps there should be some intermediate procedure which would be easier for everyone concerned:

> It imposes quite a lot on the system, having a power of arrest clause, because at the instigation of the petitioner you can have the man arrested, he is then required to be brought before a judge anywhere in the country within twenty-four hours when you suddenly require the attendance of someone on behalf of the complainant, someone on behalf of the husband, someone from the police who conducted the arrest, and the judge and the clerk and everyone else, so that is, I think, why they are so rare, because they are quite a swingeing remedy for the wife to have available, and people always bear in mind the possibility that the wife may say he's done something when he hasn't, knowing he will get arrested for it. I think if there were an intermediate procedure it would be easier — if the police were entitled to arrest and investigate themselves, and not to have to bring the defendant to the judge immediately. (Solr 5, male, Cumbria)

In fact, it seemed to be administrative convenience, rather than the "swingeing" nature of the remedy, that was this solicitor's main concern.

The question of accepting undertakings when they were offered rather than persisting with an application for a court order led to more discussion, but here again, the views of the solicitors were not completely in accord with those of their clients, administrative convenience being favoured over effectiveness. A large majority of solicitors (six out of eight) either preferred undertakings and would encourage or even pressure their clients into accepting them; or they recognised that, if not always preferable, they had certain advantages in appropriate cases, and should always be the *first* remedy to be tried. This is a selection of their comments:

> We try to resolve as many as possible by undertakings because it saves everybody's time... If you get a chap who would agree to an undertaking and the client wife says, "No, I want this thing to be heard," then I would put pressure on her not to. I would say, "This is not a reasonable use of lawyers' time. An undertaking has the same force. Everybody knows that undertakings are a way of speeding up the process and there is no smoke without fire but it's not worth hearing the evidence, it will probably cause more distress than you are bargaining for." (Solr 1, male, Bristol)

> They do seem to be a good way of alleviating the time and effort and getting some kind of enforceable promise. I sometimes feel it's quite an advantage to women because you can sometimes use it as a lever to get at things. (Solr 4, female, Bristol)

> I do actually believe it's better to get an agreement and rely on that and go straight back to court if anything goes wrong. (Solr 3, female, Bristol)

The last solicitor quoted went on to say, however:

> It may sometimes be that women feel they have a raw deal and somehow the man has got away with it, and they feel less willing to come back to court on another occasion. (Solr 3, female, Bristol)

Another solicitor, who also thought that undertakings should be tried first as "one step along the the line" to a full order, nonetheless had little confidence that such a promise would be kept at all:

> They're absolutely useless, they're there to be broken... I think the undertaking is proffered with good intentions but it is the provocation from one side or the other — it's no use talking about undertakings once the pubs have closed and he's gone back home. (Solr 8, male, Cumbria)

Only two solicitors — both working in the same practice — said unequivocally that they would *not* put any pressure on a woman to accept an undertaking of good behaviour which her husband or cohabitee had offered to the court:

> If they want a full order, I think we'd get the full order. (Solr 7, male, Cumbria)

> I don't think women are put under pressure at all. The court will look at the facts and decide whether it's fit and proper that there should be an injunction, bearing in mind that it's got a duty to both parties. (Solr 7B, male, Cumbria)

This last solicitor felt that undertakings might work very well with those he saw as "middle class clients" where "he's just boiled over the once," but that when you are "dealing with a green form type where he has perhaps got a bad history of heavy drinking and assault and all

109

the rest of it, then it's a complete waste of time." These assumptions — that the most persistent and dangerously violent men are all working class, that alcohol abuse is a working class phenomenon, and that most if not all serious assaults are associated with heavy drinking — are of course not borne out by the evidence of this study or any previous studies.

In those areas where cases which are brought to the county courts initially come before the Registrar, the pressure on the man to offer and the woman to accept an undertaking is obviously very high, since this can be formalised by the Registrar without the need to bring in the county court judge:

> Sometimes the short cut way, instead of going before a judge, you can go before the Registrar for directions. Now if the husband turns up and says, "OK, I will not use violence against my wife", he gives an undertaking to the court saying he will not use violence against her, that's as good, that can be enforced... He'll say, "I didn't hit her, it's a load of rubbish," or "She was doing this, that and the other," and you can always say, "Well, look, you haven't hit your wife and you're not going to hit your wife, so what's the harm in giving an undertaking saying you won't?" and that's where it tends to get used. It gets over the problem where one party is denying it and the wife still gets the protection she needs. (Solr 6, male, Cumbria)

(See also p100, Choice of Courts, especially quote from Solr 5 p102).

The option of substituting a promise or undertaking before the court instead of a "proper" court order is not available in the magistrates' court, therefore those solicitors who tend to use the magistrates' court for protection orders will be more inclined to advise their clients to persist with their applications, in the face of the man's denials, since the only other option is to withdraw the application altogether. The magistrates' court clerk we talked to said he felt that in most cases, undertakings were "creatures of expediency," and that there was an element of dishonesty in offering — or advising — an undertaking when the respondent insists he has done nothing wrong. He also felt that the women could often feel resentful in this kind of situation:

> I would have thought that resentment stems from (the fact that) the woman may feel that her point of view has not been given credence by the court... You're not in this situation obviously looking for reconciliation of the two parties but in a sense to conciliate their differences. You need honesty, and to me, (if) the judge in that situation explains to the man there is no acceptance of him having done anything wrong in the past, that doesn't in my view enable a conciliation process to start off... The basis on which you resolve differences is to some extent based on mutual honesty of each other's faults and acceptance of each other's faults, and I just think it's an expedient solution that just doesn't work.

It certainly seems that all the practitioners in this field have a vested interest in advocating the advantages of the system they best know and customarily use. From the point of view of the women clients we would suggest caution in the routine use of undertakings: it is apparent from our study that they are often regarded with derision by the men and with resentment by the women; they are often unenforceable (as even those solicitors who regularly use them admit); and, to advocate an undertaking as a first routine step along the road to a fully enforceable court order — perhaps with a power of arrest attached — is to ignore the feelings of the applicants, and the stress and time that is taken up in repeated visits to the solicitor and to court, while the different stages along this long road are passed through.

Service of orders

No court order is effective until it is served in person on the individual who is its subject. This applies even to orders which have been obtained *ex parte* (i.e. without notice and without the other party being present at the hearing.) When the man is in court, the order is usually sealed and served on him immediately. If, instead of an order, he agrees to make an undertaking, he will normally have the terms of his undertaking explained to him in court, and will sign it there and then, and will then be given a copy to take away with him. In all other cases, the solicitor will be responsible for having the order served on the respondent, and will usually employ process servers or private detectives to do this. An affidavit of service then has to be filed with the court, so that all is in order if the case should return to court at a later date.

> The injunction ... is actually ineffective until he has been served. It's an order that has been spoken into the air until it has been personally served on the man... Even if he so to speak breaks the order the same day or the next day, if he hasn't actually been served with the injunction, he hasn't actually broken the order at all. (Solr 3, female, Bristol)

In most cases, there is little difficulty in tracking down the man concerned, either at his home or his place of work. Often the woman can give information about his likely movements, and the places he tends to go in his leisure time. In a minority of cases, however, there is considerable difficulty in finding the man in order to effect service. Some men are deliberately elusive or may disappear completely once they suspect that trouble may be brewing. Others come and go periodically, but still manage to evade service for some considerable period, during which time the woman is completely unprotected.

Similar problems can arise in serving the man notice of the full hearing, and — once an order *has* been served, and has been subsequently broken — in serving him with notice of committal proceedings. Sometimes, when there have been persistent problems, the judge will allow "substituted service"; that is, at the suggestion of the woman's lawyers, he or she will order that a particular named individual may receive the order and/or notice of the hearing on the respondent's behalf. In other cases, the judge has ruled that "service be deemed good" as in this example.

> It wasn't certain that it had ever been served but the judge said, "I don't care, he knew what was coming, the level of violence was extremely severe and I'm not prepared to give him a second chance." Now that's the kind of trenchant approach for which the Bristol judges are excellent. If there's obviously a simple procedural irregularity which doesn't actually affect the substance of the thing, they'll make the order anyway. (Solr 1, male, Bristol)

This approach has not, to our knowledge, been used in relation to a committal hearing, however, where the courts are always at pains to ensure that the correct procedures are followed to the letter.

Enforcement of orders

As we have suggested in earlier chapters, the question of enforcement of injunctions and other court orders is a major issue. One of the problems lies in the diverging views of the court personnel on the one hand, and the women experiencing violence on the other. Whereas the court staff are of the opinion that injunctions and personal protection orders are almost always effective (since very few women ever come back to court) the women themselves are very aware of the extremely limited nature of the protection they receive. Solicitors' perceptions come somewhere between these two views. Among those we talked to, four solicitors (three of them practising in Cumbria) believed that most court orders were fairly effective from the start, because the majority of men realise, if their partners have gone to court, that the matter must be taken seriously, and they are not prepared to come into conflict with the law.

> I should say nine times out of ten, when you serve the first order on the husband, that stops it. Either it hits his pride and off he goes and leave, or it tends to do the trick actually. Nine times out of ten, you get the first order which they might do for twenty-eight days or two months, and it invariably just dies a death because usually you've got your divorce proceedings going and the whole heat goes out of the situation. (Solr 6, male, Cumbria)
> Having gone to court once, the husband realises, and once the parties are separated, the tendency to fall out is lessened and it's really only the aggressive or obstructive or awkward husbands who are the ones who persist, and ... keep coming back to the judge. (Solr 5, male, Cumbria)

Among the remaining solicitors, opinions were divided. Two solicitors specifically mentioned enforcement as one of the major problems in relation to injunctions and personal protection orders:

The problem is enforcement. You cannot get a power of arrest attached on an *ex parte*, unless there is some history. But on a one-off, not unless you've got criminal violence involved... Some of the police don't like enforcing them anyway. It just becomes part of their paperwork with which they find it difficult to cope. And the committal procedure is pretty cumbersome. (Solr 1, male, Bristol)

It isn't really protection — the actual enforcement of it is so weak and long drawn out. I don't feel it is an answer, I don't feel it is protection sometimes... Enforcement is usually so unsatisfactory that it can be an awful lot of hassle to go through for so little reward. (Solr 4, female, Bristol)

The last solicitor quoted felt that most judges did not take breaches of non-molestation and exclusion orders seriously enough. She felt that it was important to take any breach back to court immediately (if the woman wished to) rather than, as some solicitors do, merely writing a letter to the offending man as a first step. Another solicitor felt that magistrates were even less likely than judges to take a breach of an order seriously, but that they were perhaps getting better than they used to be.

If you go before the magistrates, the men tend to say, "I'm very sorry, I won't let it happen again, and the magistrates tend to let them off... They seem rather loth to send someone to prison because he's in breach... Now the magistrates have got used to doing them, it's better. I think when they first started, they were a bit wishy washy about them. (Solr 6, male, Cumbria)

This solicitor's view that judges have "a bit more confidence and (are) used to sending people away for things like that" does not, however, seem to be borne out in practice: from our observations and the comments of those solicitors (mostly in Bristol) who agreed that judges were reluctant to commit for a civil offence, it seemed that most committal applications which got as far as the court room seemed to end up with a warning, and perhaps the addition of a power of arrest to the original order, only. And this is not taking into account the many breaches which are never reported to a court because the solicitor feels that the incident was a relatively minor one.

It may be that solicitors' reluctance to return to court is related to their understanding that committal applications are complicated and need to be exactly right (a view which was expressed by five solicitors in all).

Unless your notices are in the prescribed form, you don't get your committal. There have been too many cases recently where an error has

113

been made, and so long as you have someone astute enough on the other side, your committal goes out the window and is scrapped and you have to reapply. (Solr 2, male, Bristol)

Yes, of course, committals, they must know exactly what the guy has been arraigned for and the courts are very particular about the (need) to show cause, it should be on the prescribed form and itemised exactly how he's broken the injunction and the facts supporting it, that's only proper. (Solr 7B, male, Cumbria)

The committal procedures are pretty cumbersome... It's the same difficulty I mentioned before. If you're going to have a legal system that allows everybody to have their point ,of view, you've got to have a committal procedure which allows the other side, the chap, to make his case. I think it's rare, but you do get the odd malicious woman whose case is not well-founded, and who is determined to get hubby behind bars, even though there's not much merit in it. I think it's rare but it happens. (Solr 1, male, Bristol)

The reluctance to send men to prison for domestic assaults is, as we have seen, shared by the women themselves. It may be that imprisonment is not the best way to deal with offences of any kind. What is clear, however, is that this lenient, almost laissez faire, approach to dealing with breaches of court orders gives the impression, to both the woman and the man, that the orders themselves are a bit of a joke, and can be ignored with impunity. Neither the safety of the woman nor the authority of the court is being respected, so long as this situation continues.

The Police

When a man breaches a court order, it is often out of office hours, and it may therefore be impossible for the woman to get in touch with her solicitor immediately. In most cases, whether or not there is a power of arrest attached to the order, she will call on the police in the first instance, but, as we have seen, their response is often less than satisfactory. Four of the solicitors we talked to had some reservations about police practices. Two felt that the police should often do much more than they did, and one of them remarked also that in her experience, many police officers made racist comments and were perhaps even less helpful to black women than to white ones. One solicitor felt that the police needed "educating" regarding undertakings and should perhaps be encouraged to enforce a power of arrest if one had been attached. Criticisms of the police were both stronger and more common among Bristol solicitors than those in Cumbria.

I know the police are supposed to be doing more. I think they should be doing a lot more. It seems crazy that they treat domestic situations different from any other violent situation, even if it does mean more

114

work for them. (Solr 2, male, Bristol)
I think if there was more police back-up throughout, certainly once an injunction has been got, then I think they would be more respected by men and valued by women... I'm sure the police's attitude towards domestic violence is probably even more hopeless in the case of black families. (Solr 3, female, Bristol)

Solicitors in Cumbria were much more likely to accept that the police might not want to get involved in domestic situations, and even that this reluctance was understandable. One solicitor, for example, suggested that only if there were a divorce or a legal separation in progress would he feel justified in requesting some police involvement:

(The police) are helpful in cases where strong representations are made to them that this is not a domestic situation where they are likely to have their fingers burnt. I would have to weigh up quite carefully whether my client was going to be determined to remain away from him because I would lose credibility with the local police force ... if on occasion I have a client who says, "This is desperately urgent, you must do something now," and I put myself out on a limb by telling the police officers, "This is a lady who is going to run all the way, and complains of assault, she is not going to withdraw the statement," and then a week later she is back with him and says, "I don't want to go on with it." (Solr 5, male, Cumbria)

Another solicitor in the same area also said that he found it understandable that the police were very reluctant to get involved in domestic disputes, especially when they were called out to the same families week after week.

A slightly different kind of complaint was that the police tended to want women to go for powers of arrest when this was not always appropriate:

You've got to view this in the context of the social milieu, if you like. What happens is that the lady gets beaten up or the lady has a problem. She rings for the police, the police say, "Oh, it's a domestic, we don't want to know," but they will turn up, and the first thing the police say to the little lady is, "Go and see your solicitor, go and get an injunction with powers of arrest, and then we'll be able to put him in the slammer." So the lady is pre-programmed to come to the door and say, whether it's appropriate or not, "We want power of arrest, and we want an injunction." Now you can't have automatic power of arrest because there would be injustice in that. (Solr 7B, male, Cumbria)

Our two interviews with police officers confirmed that an order from a civil court is not taken particularly seriously by them, unless a power of arrest is attached. Both tended to advocate (criminal) prosecution in the first instance, if the injuries constituted ABH or

115

worse.

> The difficulty when it comes to domestic violence is, if you arrest somebody who has maybe come in drunk and his wife makes a complaint, she has injuries and we will charge him. The following morning, he's bailed and they make it up and she doesn't want any further action... And then the CPS won't pursue it. (Police officer)

This officer also felt that all injunctions should have a power of arrest attached, or they were meaningless and could not be effective:

> I think all injunctions should have a power of arrest to get the person away from the woman. You must have the power of arrest to get that person in front of court next morning. (Police officer)

The other officer (who is now retired) said he would be extremely reluctant to take any action which might lead to the break up of a marriage, especially if there were any children involved. He went on to say that if a woman called them out but, when they arrived, the man refused them entrance, they would usually withdraw:

> The assaults invariably take place inside the dwelling of another. I mean the Englishman's home is his castle, so to speak. Police officers, particular modern time police officers, are very very reticent about going in a dwelling house unless they know there's a serious assault taking place, because if the wife rings up and says, "I want you to come up here, I'm being seriously assaulted," and the policeman goes to the door and the husband stands there — not the wife, the wife's in the bedroom, he's told her to stop where she is — and he says, "You're not coming in, we've just had a tiff, you're *not coming in* here," now then we're on dicey ground... You've got the possibility of a suing, the Chief Constable being sued for unlawful trespass... so whether or not the law should be stretched to allow the police more powers to do that without them being held to this with a writ of some sort, I don't know. I tend to think no, it shouldn't. (Retired police officer)

In this man's view, even the existence of a court order would make little difference unless the woman's solicitor had requested police involvement. Clearly this practice is totally unacceptable and shows an erroneous understanding of the existing legal position, and we would hope that it is no longer being followed in the area concerned. Nonetheless, even where police practice does not so blatantly contradict all the established guidelines, there is still an enormous gulf between what women need to ensure their safety (and feel they are entitled to) and what, in most cases, they get from the officers sent in response to their call for help.

Rural areas

We have already alluded to some of the problems faced by women

116

living in rural areas, and wish simply to reiterate them here. Firstly, in such areas, neither the judges nor the magistrates sit every day, so that the courts are likely to be much less accessible in an emergency than they are in towns and cities. This may mean that *ex parte* orders are less easily obtainable and that as much as ten days notice may be required. Magistrates tend to be more frequently available than judges on a regular basis, and more prepared to hear applications at times when the court would not normally be sitting, so this leads to proportionately more use of the magistrates' courts legislation in rural areas. (Since this legislation only applies to married women, there is a good case for amending it in line with the DVA, to enable the courts to be more accessible to cohabitees in rural areas.) Because the judge may visit the area only once or twice a month, registrars tend to hear initial applications in the county court, so a process of "screening" occurs, which is not the usual practice in urban areas.

The second main problem in rural areas is the lack of alternative accommodation, and the associated difficulties couples face in avoiding each other if both wish to stay in same local area. As against this, there may in some cases be more support from family and friends, who are perhaps more likely to live near at hand and feel able to offer help and perhaps somewhere to stay.

Thirdly, professionals in rural areas may be unaccustomed to being consulted by women facing domestic violence, and this lack of experience may mean that they deal with such cases less effectively. There also appeared to be a readiness among the people we spoke to in Cumbria to accept some of the discredited myths about domestic violence — for example, that it is wrong to interfere between man and wife, or that the women are accustomed to the beatings and don't really want to do anything about it. Attitudes of this kind seem to be rather less common among professional workers in urban areas. One woman now working in a refuge in Cumbria explained to us:

> I lived in (a small village) myself for ages and I must admit I felt rather isolated there. It was a case of sticking in and getting on with it, and they're still doing that... Thinking back to my own (experience), when I had young kiddies and wasn't terribly happy, basically there is nothing, you talk to the doctor, talk to the vicar, and you know, "Never mind, dear, everybody goes through it," and I think that's still going on in rural areas.

This combination of lack of experienced advisers, unhelpful attitudes and the relative inaccessibility of courts, refuges and other alternatives make it very difficult for women in areas like this to find a solution to their difficulties, when their partners treat them abusively.

Black women

In spite of specific questioning on this subject, only one solicitor, practising in Bristol, talked at any length about the additional kinds of help and support which might be needed by black women, and the particular problems they might face. This solicitor made a number of points, some of which we will take up in the recommendations in our concluding chapter. Her general view was that the legal system is not very accessible or accommodating to black people, and that, as a result, black women (and men) will only tend to consult a solicitor when they can see no other alternative. Black women who are experiencing violence in their relationships will initially try to deal with it themselves or within their own communities, and will only use the law as a last resort:

> The clients I've had who have been black have tended to... experience far greater and more long-lasting violence than the white women. Why that is so I'm not sure, but the level of violence has been so extreme and has continued for so long... that I suppose I would guess ... that there are some black relationships that are very violent... where there are social conditions which produce situations which are very upset and distraught... And black clients have said to me, "I don't want to take this to court because the black community has already got a bad enough name... I'm really hesitant about taking him to court at all, I've tried to deal with it in the community"... So I suspect that with black women, it's going on a lot more and I'm not seeing the clients, they're not wanting to come..." (Solr 3, female, Bristol)

She went on to say that Asian women, in particular, were often frightened to involve a solicitor, for fear that their partners would react even more violently when threatened with legal action.

This solicitor felt that there was a need for more black lawyers, for black legal information and advice services, and for a fully funded and accessible interpreting service which would be available for individual solicitors and at court.

> Just to have more black visibility, I think, within the court system, that would make such a difference. There are almost no black solicitors around, and the one that leaps to mind is a man and frequently acting for men. So that wouldn't, I think, be an encouragement for black women to go to him. Maybe for solicitors like us, we are not black but nonetheless working in this field, to go out to black groups more and talk about how injunctions work and what could be done and whether they're effective... Just to get the message out that this is available and perhaps get the support of the local community to support women who take this action. (Solr 3, female, Bristol)

We endorse all these points and would give our full support to any development of specific services for black women.

General comments on injunctions, personal protection orders and the court system

The solicitors we talked to had rather mixed feelings about the value of injunctions and other court orders. They recognised that the woman's main aim, in preventing further abuse, was not always achieved, though their estimations of the likely success rate were rather more optimistic than our own.

> It is a very rough and ready system. It's good as far as it goes but it's not really as good as it might be, to be honest, and enforcement is a problem, in fact I think it's probably the major problem because you do get the odd chap who just says "Up yours" to injunctions. (Solr 1, male, Bristol)

Two solicitors, both women, felt that even if the man did not comply with an order totally, the very fact that the woman had gone through with her application and the court had applied sanctions could in itself give her confidence and help to empower her, thus changing the relationship for the better.

> I think (a non-molestation order) can stir up a lot of trouble, but I think it can also make the man realise there is some kind of sanction. I think... even if it may not necessarily improve the physical circumstances of the woman, ... it can be an empowering thing to do, to get the court to say that that is (unacceptable). (Solr 4, female, Bristol)

Most of the solicitors' other criticisms were directed at the court process itself, and this seemed to be almost exclusively the concern of Bristol practitioners. The practice whereby Friday is "injunction day" in Bristol county court led to some comment. Solicitors felt that this practice was more to the advantage of lawyers than their clients. The over-crowded and tense conditions (detailed earlier) were a result in part of this concentration of injunction applications on one day, and indicated that, ideally, at least two days should be set aside for this. Moreover the pressure to complete all applications that day could sometimes be a problem, and it could be difficult either effecting service or protecting women during the immediately following weekend. On the other hand, some solicitors felt that when women consulted them earlier in the week, it was quite helpful to be able to work up to Friday as a culmination of the injunction application process. Clearly, there are points to be made both for and against this practice, but given the pressure on court time, and the apparently growing number of applications, having two regular "injunction days" in Bristol and comparable cities, would seem to be desirable, and more judges should be available to hear urgent cases promptly, even when a lengthy contested hearing is anticipated.

Conclusion

In this chapter, we have concentrated particularly on the views of the solicitors, as the group of professionals whose contact both with women experiencing domestic violence, and the court system, is most crucial. Solicitors share many of the same reservations as their clients concerning the effectiveness of court orders and the need for stricter enforcement; they are also equally critical of the poor facilities and cramped waiting areas offered by many courts. Many of them are also severely critical of the lack of back-up provided by the police.

Solicitors' perceptions differ from their clients in regard to their emphasis on the need for both sides to have a equal hearing. Understandably, women who have experienced violence and abuse at the hands of their partners are less inclined to put much credence on men's property rights, when it is their own safety and that of their children which is at stake. Solicitors are also more likely to regard the process of the law as "fair" (or at least aiming to be fair) whereas women themselves feel disadvantaged from the outset.

The other issue relates to solicitors general attitudes and manner in relating to their clients. While several solicitors spoke sympathetically about the need to reassure the women who consulted them, and to explain the various options to them fully, women themselves often felt they were not receiving the reassurance and clear explanations which they needed. There is no doubt that some solicitors treat their clients in a very patronising and sometimes supercilious manner. Some of them subscribe to invalid stereotypes about "battered women" being inarticulate, of low intelligence, passive, and unwilling to do anything effective to change the situation. Their help and advice is therefore given half-heartedly in the expectation that the woman will soon return to her violent partner; and if this expectation is fulfilled, there is little understanding of the pressures which might have led to this outcome. It should be remembered that the solicitors who were willing to talk at length to us on these questions are likely to be among the *most* sympathetic of their profession, and the many solicitors who are unrepresented in our sample are more likely to hold anti-women attitudes.

With regard to other professionals, our sample was even less representative so no general conclusions can be drawn. We would like to point out, however, that there is a clear need for more education and training to be directed particularly to voluntary groups (such as Citizens' Advice Bureaux, and Victim Support) and to the police regarding the issues involved, and the other kinds of help and support that are, or should be, available.

Footnotes

1. ABWOR means assistance by way of representation. It is a way of extending the Green Form scheme to cover going to the domestic magistrates' court, but it does not cover county court or high court proceedings. It is cheaper and simpler than applying for full legal aid.

CHAPTER 7:
CONCLUSION

Introduction
The findings we have presented here came from a small exploratory study of the extent to which the legal system can provide effective protection against violence from partners and ex-partners. Domestic violence is covered by both civil and criminal law; but the latter focuses attention on the offender, and can provide, at best, only indirect benefit for those who are the victims and survivors of the abuse. The main concern of this report is therefore the civil legislation, and, in particular, court orders (injunctions and personal protection orders) for which women can apply, in an attempt to prevent further molestation, sometimes by excluding their partners from the home.

As detailed earlier (see Chapter 1), the methods used in this study included court observations, and interviews with women who have experienced domestic violence, and with a small number of solicitors and other individuals whose paid or voluntary work includes some responsibility for advising and supporting women in this situation. In this chapter, we will summarise our main findings, and consider some of the implications for any future legislative change or reform of associated procedures, and for future research in this area.

Limitations on Domestic Violence Legislation
There are certain categories of abused women who fall outside the the criteria of the existing legislation — e.g. former spouses (except, in certain circumstances, where there are children), ex-cohabitants, and those who have never lived with their abuser. Women also find it difficult or impossible to obtain protection from their violent teenage or adult sons.

In such cases, the usual procedure is a "tort" action for damages and/or trespass. This has to be initiated as "a peg to hang the injunction on" — as the applicant's lawyers frequently stated in court. This seems to lead to unnecessary complications, which sometimes mean adjourning the damages hearing indefinitely (since only rarely are women seriously wanting financial compensation, but are simply seeking protection.)

An additional problem is that powers of arrest cannot be added to such an injunction.

We believe that the legislation should be amended so that, whatever the woman's marital status, relationship to her abuser, or living arrangements, she would be able to get protection under the same legislation, in either a magistrates' or a county court.

Undertakings

In the county court (though not in the magistrates' court) the practice of accepting a sworn undertaking from the woman's aggressor, as a substitute for a court order, is extremely common. Many lawyers, it seems, prefer this practice, on the grounds that it reduces bitterness and underlines the man's responsibility for his actions. It is also quicker and more convenient for the courts, as it obviates the need for a lengthy contested hearing, and registrars as well as judges are empowered to accept such undertakings.

In principle, undertakings have the same force as a court order, and a man can be brought back to court and committed for breach of an undertaking in the same way as he can be for breach of an injunction. In practice, however, they are more likely to be disregarded, not only by the men (who feel they have got off lightly) but by police officers and the courts who may be called upon later to enforce them. We do not deny that, in some cases, an undertaking may be appropriate; (if, for example, the violence was a one-off incident, and both parties agree that it is very unlikely to happen again). We are, however, concerned by the situation in which women are often made to feel they have no choice in the matter, even though they believe — with good reason — that their partner will not keep to the terms of any promise he makes to the court.

Overall there often seems to be too much emphasis on coming to an amicable agreed settlement. This is perhaps a reaction to excessively litigious divorce cases in the past, but is now taken to extremes (and the current proposals from the Law Commission regarding a "genuine" no-fault divorce legislation reinforce this.) The result is that many women, even if they finally obtain their injunctions or protection orders, and the man obeys them, still feel that the whole process is not worth the trouble it caused; they still feel frightened, they often feel aggrieved, and many of them say they would never go through it all over again, whatever happened.

We believe it should be recognised that where one party has been physically violent or severely abusive, the concept of "no fault" is dishonest and unrealistic, and creates an injustice whereby the least powerful partner is penalised. In such cases, it is necessary for the court to "take sides" against the violent

partner, and to demonstrate — by making a strong order or by committing a defaulting partner to prison — that such behaviour is never acceptable, and will always be taken seriously.

Exclusion orders

In every case in our study, women who applied for non-molestation orders were successful in receiving either an order or an equivalent undertaking (though we have already indicated our unease at this substitution; see above, p123). Exclusion applications were more problematic, however. Almost never was an exclusion order granted *ex parte*, except where the man had already left the home (or had never lived there) and had no rights of residence. (The magistrates' court has no power to grant expedited exclusion orders, and because — under the existing legislation — the parties would always be married, both would have equal rights of occupation of the marital home.) In the vast majority of cases, the exclusion application was adjourned until the full hearing which, in the county court, was usually the next week, but in the magistrates' court, could be several weeks away.

This waiting time could in itself cause considerable problems, if the woman and her children had no safe place to go in the meantime. These difficulties were exacerbated if, on the return date, the solicitor reported that the man had not yet been served with notice of the hearing; or that he had been served, but had failed to turn up. Judges have power to abridge time for service, or even to "deem" that "service has been effected" if considerable efforts have been made to find the man, and it is felt he is deliberately evading service. Some judges were more likely to use these powers than others. (One judge we talked to said that, in extreme cases, if he were approached in the morning, he would order immediate service of the notice, and hear the case "*ex parte* on notice" that afternoon; i.e. the man would technically have been given notice of the hearing, but was unlikely to be present because of the shortness of the notice given. In his view, this was preferable to an immediate *ex parte* hearing.)

A further problem is that, even if the man is present, if he contests the exclusion application, and/or asks for time to find alternative accommodation, the order is unlikely to take effect immediately, and may not be granted at all. Legally, there is a considerable difference between an order warning against assault or molestation (i.e. preventing an offence) and one depriving a person of a legal right, for example, to occupy property of which one is (co-)owner or tenant. In practice, however, the one is unlikely to be effective without the other; and from the woman's point of view, a simple non-molestation order is useless since it does not allow her to return and remain unmolested in what is, after all, *her* home, too.

We therefore recommend that, if a woman needs her partner to be excluded to ensure her protection, the application should be heard without delay, and without the need to serve notice on her partner.

Exclusion orders and Custody

A particular case of this general reluctance to grant exclusion orders relates to the custody of any children of the relationship. Some judges are reluctant, or completely refuse, to grant exclusion orders if both parties are contesting custody, care and control. This is on the grounds that to leave the woman in the house with the children, while excluding the (violent) man would "prejudge" the custody issue. However, the custody hearing cannot normally be heard for several weeks, (or even months) and a simple non–molestation order is in most cases *not* sufficient protection.

While we accept that the man may sometimes be justified in contesting custody, and we would not wish to deprive him of his right to do so, we believe that in some cases this is simply a ploy to delay his exclusion. We are also, of course, concerned that the woman is at serious risk of further violence while the issue is pending.

The problem here is the presumption that whichever parent has interim care and control will be preferred when permanent custody orders are decided. (This presumption also works against women if they have had to leave their children behind temporarily when leaving a violent or abusive relationship). However, provided regular access (at specified times) can be arranged, there seems to be no reason other than custom to maintain this general practice, which seems to privilege the father, and does not benefit either the mother, or the children.

We recommend that a pending custody application should never be seen as, in itself, an adequate reason to delay an ouster application.

Enforcement of Injunctions and Protection Orders.

This is a real problem, which is not adequately appreciated by judges, magistrates or solicitors. It is certainly our view that many more court orders are broken than ever come to the attention of any court.

The problem has a number of components:
a)   the reluctance of judges and magistrates to add power of arrest to court orders.
b)   police reluctance to act *without* having a power of arrest, or even, in

125

some cases, when it has been added.
c) solicitors' reluctance to take men back to court for "minor" breaches.
d) courts' reluctance to commit a man until he has breached an injunction repeatedly.

We would like to recommend that:

(i) **power of arrest should be added as a** *general rule* **whenever there has been ABH.** It would then be up to the man (or his legal representatives) to demonstrate conclusively that it is *not* necessary, otherwise it should be automatically added. (This was recommended by the Women's National Commission in their Select Committee Report (1985) but this recommendation has never been acted upon.)

(ii) **if a man is clearly in breach of an order which has power of arrest attached, it should be the norm (rather than merely permissible) for the police to arrest him.**

(iii) **if, unusually, there was no power of arrest, the police should always arrest is there is evidence of an assault, and in all circumstances should remove the man from the premises and (separately) advise the woman of her rights and take her to a place of safety if she so wishes.**

The question of prosecution is more questionable, since it may not always benefit the woman, especially if adequate protection cannot be provided for her while the case is pending. This does not, however, preclude an initial arrest, even if the charge is later dropped.

(iv) **if the man is in breach of an order, and has been brought back to court,** *even if he is a first offender* he should be treated severely, as a deterrent both to himself and to others. A prison sentence — albeit only for a few days in the first instance — should be regarded as the norm, and it should be up to the man (or his legal advisers) to argue conclusively that this not appropriate in this case.

(This is recommended in the knowledge that most women do not tell their solicitors of minor breaches, and most solicitors react to the first such breach of which they are informed by writing to the husband's solicitor with a warning. Therefore, once a breach comes to court, it is usually (a) serious and (b) the culmination of a series of infringements, and therefore hardly a "first offence" to be treated leniently.)

Solicitors

Women had two major complaints against their solicitors. Firstly, they were concerned that their solicitors did not explain everything fully to them, in a way that they could understand. At the initial visit, a woman may be extremely upset and bewildered, and have no idea what can be done, or even what she *wants* to do. She may therefore be unable to take a lot of new information in very quickly. Her solicitor must take this into account and be particularly careful to explain the various options available to her as clearly and simply as possible, and not rush into making a decision she may later regret. At later stages in the legal process, also, solicitors often seemed to decide on a particular course of action, without fully consulting the woman client about whether she wishes to take that action or not. At court, for example, "deals" were often worked out between the lawyers representing the two opposing sides, without the clients being fully conversant with what was going on. **We believe that solicitors should consult their clients carefully at all stages, and should not pressure them into making a decision hastily without full consideration of alternative courses of action.**

The second complaint relates to the adequacy of the advice that is given and the actions which are taken. In certain cases, it was patently clear that a woman had been given erroneous information and advice; for example, one woman was told she would not be able to get an injunction of any kind because the man who was harassing her was her ex-husband, who had not lived with her for several years. Another woman was advised to agree to sell the house she and her husband owned jointly. This was before any date had been fixed for a property adjustment hearing; as a result, she was left homeless, while her husband was able to buy a new house in his sole name, and on which she apparently had no claim. Other solicitors took an unnecessarily long time before bringing an application to court, so that the woman began to lose hope that anything would ever get done.

We would like to endorse the recommendation made by Lorna Smith in her report to the Home Office (1989): that local law societies draw up lists of solicitors who are experienced in the intricacies of domestic violence law, and make these lists available to organisations such as CABx, libraries, law centres and community centres. We suggest also that additional information should be included; for example, whether a solicitor's office is accessible to those in wheelchairs, which languages are spoken, whether interpreters and signers are available, and whether solicitors are prepared to make home visits to clients with disabilities. Published lists of this kind would help women to find their way to an appropriate solicitor who would take action quickly.

We would also like to suggest that solicitors undertaking this work give some thought to the possibility of working with Women's Aid to produce one or more leaflets or pamphlets on "What to expect when you go to court" and "What is an injunction/personal protection order". These could be given to women who consulted them regarding domestic violence, and would be available for them to refer to at any time during the proceedings. This would not, of course, obviate the need for a reassuring and unhurried reception and first interview: **it is of prime importance that all solicitors who make it known that they welcome domestic violence work should have a sympathetic and reassuring manner, and feel able to give adequate time to answering all the woman's questions.**

Waiting at court

Going to court can be extremely distressing, and this is exacerbated by the lack of adequate facilities at most courts. People often have to wait in very crowded smoky conditions, sometimes for many hours, as only rarely, it seems, are definite appointments made and kept. Most courts do not make it easy for women to avoid coming into contact with their partners. Often there are no separate rooms for private discussions with legal advisers, and there may be no refreshments or toilet facilities, and almost certainly, nowhere for children to go. If a woman has arranged for her children to be cared for elsewhere, she may be worried about them if the wait is longer than she anticipated; and older children may need to be picked up from school at midday or during the course of the afternoon.

While the hearing itself is bound to be fairly stressful in some ways, there are things that could be done to make the whole process easier, and in particular to make the waiting time more comfortable. We feel that the following suggestions would be worth considering, though we recognise that not all of them could be implemented immediately.

a) **it is essential that there are enough separate interview rooms and waiting areas to allow (i) private consultation with legal advisers, welfare officers, etc. (ii) privacy while waiting — separate from partner (iii) both smoking and non-smoking areas.**

b) **wherever possible, an appointments system should operate so that women do not have to wait around all day.** This not only adds considerably to the stress of it all, but leads to practical problems regarding child care and taking time off work.

c) **refreshments should be available** — preferably from human beings rather than machines. There should be a choice of both hot and cold drinks, which recognises different cultural and dietary needs.

d) **toilets and baby changing areas should not only exist but be adequately signposted.**

e) a *friendly* receptionist/usher/enquiry person should be present, both in the foyer and evident in the waiting areas.(In magistrates' courts particularly it seems to be assumed that everyone know the procedure, and there is often no one around to ask where to go, etc.)

f) **it may be worth thinking about having a children's play area and someone to look after the children where parents are unable to make their own arrangements.** (In one case, the court usher, in another, a woman police officer, and in a third, an articled clerk were persuaded to look after babies and small children. In other cases, children were taken into the court room.)

In Court

The procedure inside the court room itself varies according to whether the hearing is at a county court before a judge (or occasionally a registrar); or at a magistrates' court, in front of three or more Justices of Peace from the domestic panel. In the county court, the evidence is given by sworn affidavit, and the petitioner and respondent will only be called upon to give oral evidence in person if the application is contested or the evidence disputed. In the magistrates' court, the applicant and the respondent are asked to give their stories in their own words to the bench.

We believe that, ideally, there should be some compromise between these two procedures. The magistrates' court procedure can be nerve-wracking and time-consuming. Many women feel intimidated by having to talk about such intimate matters before five or six people whom they do not know, and who have power to determine things which will affect their lives. They may not do themselves justice, and sometimes they are uncertain how much detail, or which details are relevant and will help their case.

In the county court, the woman's solicitor or barrister normally presents the case briefly, and she will not be called at all unless there have been further incidents since the affidavit was sworn, or her partner's lawyers or the judge wishes to cross examine her. The woman may therefore feel both mystified and disempowered by the whole procedure, which is *about* her but in which she, literally, has no say. This is especially frustrating if — as sometimes happens — the solicitor/barrister gets certain crucial details, like dates and names, wrong, leaves out vital points, or fails to press her case insistently enough.

In both cases, domestic violence cases are normally heard in chambers, in order to ensure privacy. This has a number of advantages, but also means that normally only the applicant herself, and her lawyer(s), and her partner and his lawyer(s) are allowed into court [1]. Some women might want to take a friend or relative with them into court (or perhaps a Women's Aid worker or a volunteer from another agency) and we believe this should be permissible even if the hearing is in chambers. (The attitudes of those accompanying a woman are very important, however, and when support is provided by agencies which have little experience of domestic violence, some form of training is essential.)

In contrast, cases brought in tort, and committals, are in open court, notwithstanding the intimate nature of some of the evidence. We suggest that perhaps the judge should be able to exercise discretion in closing courts to the general public when such a case is in session.

Choice between Courts

Different legislation allows both the magistrates courts and the county courts (and in certain circumstances, the High Court) powers to protect women by means of court orders. In some respects, the jurisdictions overlap; but the magistrates' courts legislation is rather more restrictive, and, in particular, is only available to married couples.

The choice of which court to use is often made by solicitors to accommodate to local and other extraneous factors (e.g. availability of sittings, known attitudes of local judges, prejudice, custom, whether or not they can get legal aid for a particular action) rather than strictly according to the merits of the case, or what would best suit the woman concerned. This is particularly important at present since the procedures in the two courts are so different (see preceding section). If our recommendations regarding standardising court procedures were put into effect, there would still be the question of the different legislative powers of judges and magistrates.

We therefore believe that the respective powers of magistrates and judges in this area of legislation should be brought into line so that whichever forum is chosen, the woman's chance of getting the protection she needs is not jeopardised. This means, for example, that the magistrates' courts legislation should be extended to apply to unmarried cohabiting couples, and that it should also be effective against harassment and molestation as well as physical violence and threats. **We also recommend** (see above, p123) **that both courts should be able to use the same legislation to protect unmarried non-cohabiting women. Exclusion orders should in**

130

principle be available *ex parte* in both court systems. Finally, the procedure for enforcement of orders should be standardised and made as effective and straightforward as possible.

Shortage of Court Time

In Bristol, and, presumably, in many other areas, the county court lists are extremely full, so that, on many occasions, a space could not be found for a contested case (which could take several hours, or most of a day) for two or three weeks or more. In most cases, it seemed that court rooms would have been available, but that there was a shortage of personnel (judges and court clerks). Whether this is an absolute lack, or due to the relatively low priority that is given to domestic injunction applications, it certainly created a problem for many women who, as a result, sometimes felt under pressure to "settle" for an undertaking, which could be agreed more quickly, or, in certain cases, could be made by a Registrar rather than a judge. (This second option was most usually usually resorted to in Kendal. See also our comments on undertakings, above.)

It is possible that some of the pressure on county court time could be alleviated if our suggested reforms regarding magistrates' courts legislation and procedures were to be implemented. This might mean that solicitors might be more inclined to use the magistrates' courts if they could be assured of an early and sympathetic hearing. **We also suggest, however, that the level of recruitment of both judges and court clerks should be examined with a view to increasing the numbers entering these professions.**

Use of the Criminal Law

We have talked very little about the possibility of criminal prosecution of violent men. This is because we feel that, as a means of *protection,* prosecution is very limited, as neither the process nor the outcome is under the control of the woman herself. In our study, the partners of only two of the women we talked to were undergoing criminal prosecution. Both cases took several months to come to court, and during that time, the man was out on bail subject to the condition that he not try to contact the woman he had assaulted. In both cases, the woman felt that the bail conditions were as effective as an injunction, and that the police would act more swiftly if these conditions were broken than if a civil order had been breached. Nonetheless, bail conditions of this kind should not be seen as a *substitute* for a civil court order, since once the case has been heard, the conditions no longer apply, and in all probability the man will merely be fined and is then free to return home. In several of the observed court cases, it was clear that a criminal prosecution was pending, but the woman and her solicitor and the judge were all agreed that an injunction — often with power of arrest — was also necessary, to carry on beyond the criminal court hearing. We see the two sets of proceedings as complementary to each other, and the existence of bail conditions should not preclude any other application going ahead in the civil courts.

It is important that, if a prosecution is undertaken, the interests of the woman and her children and in particular their safety, should be paramount. This is particularly crucial where the couple are continuing to live in. the same house. The woman's wishes regarding proceeding with prosecution should always be taken into account, and the practice of subpoena-ing her as a "hostile witness" if she wishes to withdraw seems to us highly questionable.

The main benefit of prosecution seems to us symbolic, in indicating that violence to women and children, whether within the domestic setting or not, is totally unacceptable. As Lorna Smith states:

> The criminal law ... is a normative statement. It sets the of acceptable behaviour. It is a statement of how people ought to behave and what will happen if they do not do so. (Smith, 1989, p.89)

She goes on, however, to state that:

> But if codes of behaviour set by the law are frequently broken, and there is little enforcement of the law, then the message conveyed may be that the behaviour proscribed by the law is not really worth bothering about. (*ibid*, p.89.)

This is also applicable to the civil courts' response to breach of injunctions, undertakings and personal protection orders. We feel that, at present, the police, the Crown Prosecution Service, and the civil and criminal courts do not treat male violence to women with sufficient seriousness. The message which is being put across to the men who are the perpetrators of the violence is therefore a very mixed one, and it is hardly surprising that many of them take advantage of this judicial leniency and ambivalence, and continue to assault their partners with impunity, whereas the women themselves lose all faith in the legal system, and look to other means to protect themselves. **There seems to be a considerable need for training on the issue of violence against women, for all involved in the prosecution process.**

Even when men are sent to prison, either as a result of prosecution or for a breach of an injunction, it is important to recognise that this is unlikely to be a final solution to the problem for the woman. Sooner or later (and in most cases very soon) the man will be released, and he will then be free to carry on assaulting or molesting his partner. Sometimes, he may see the woman as responsible for initiating the court process which led to his imprisonment, and he may therefore act angrily and violently towards her on his release. On the other hand, as with court orders, some men are brought up short by the sudden realisation that their partners have the power to send them to prison, and will do so if they persist in their unacceptable behaviour. To that extent, imprisonment may be an effective remedy in some cases, but, like all legal measures, this effectiveness is very limited and conditional.

The role of Women's Aid

Given the very limited effectiveness of the law, the role of Women's Aid is vital in ensuring women's safety. In the first place, Women's Aid groups throughout the country run refuges where women and their children can go to escape from their violent partners, either for a short period while they are awaiting their court hearings, or simply for a break, or for a longer period while awaiting rehousing, in cases where a court order is inappropriate, and perhaps the man has breached previous orders. The demand for refuge spaces is enormous, and far outstrips the available places. Refuges need secure funding both for the houses and for support staff. Refuge provision is also very patchy, and funds are needed to encourage groups to set up refuges in other parts of the country.

Refuges are essential, but Women's Aid offers far more than simply accommodation. Most groups have considerable experience of *all* the complex issues related to domestic violence, and can offer advice and support to women who may be considering the various options available to them, whether or not they seek refuge. Given the inadequacy of much of the legal advice available, the unwelcoming nature of the courts, and the difficulties and delays in regard to re-housing and obtaining financial provision (e.g. from D.S.S.) the need for the kind of support Women's Aid workers and volunteers offer is very evident. Women's Aid groups are also involved in training staff for other agencies — such as police and social services — in the appropriate practices and procedures when approached for help and advice by those subjected to domestic violence. Inter-agency co-operation is essential, and joint training programmes should perhaps be offered to all agencies involved. Again, our very limited resources preclude this being available on the scale it is needed.

Because refuges need to keep their locations and telephone numbers confidential, there are considerable problems in advertising their services locally. For this reason, WAFE run a national Helpline (whose number is widely publicised) which can put women in touch with the network of Women's Aid groups and refuges throughout the country. This Helpline — which is run by one paid Co-ordinator and volunteers

— is funded from donations, so again lack of resources and secure funding means that an essential service is constantly at risk of closure.

Even if all the recommendations in our report were to be put into effect immediately, there would still be a need for Women's Aid groups and refuges and a national Helpline as a contact point. The Helpline is particularly important for women in those areas of the country where there is no local refuge or Women's Aid group. Women's Aid, as the specialist organisation in this field, also has a continuing role in advocacy and training of other statutory and voluntary agencies.

Research implications

Limited resources were also responsible for many of the short-comings of this research study. As we have detailed earlier, much of our time at the beginning of the study was spent in effecting access to closed court hearings, and in recruiting one or more co-workers who could explore the particular experience of black women. The building of a sample of women (both black and white) takes considerable time, especially if it is not to be drawn exclusively from refuges, and the relatively small number of respondents is a reflection of the restricted time-scale within which we were operating. Finally, the limited geographical spread and the fact that most of our cases came from within the Bristol area means that many questions remain unanswered.

On the other hand, as a feasibility study, our research has demonstrated that the approach we have used has considerable potential if resources could be made available for a much larger project, over a longer period of time, covering many more geographical areas. It is clear even from this study, as well as from previous research (NWAF, 1980; Murch *et al.*, 1987), that court practices differ considerably from area to area and court to court. These variations need monitoring so that eventually there could be agreed guidelines which, while taking account of local conditions, nonetheless move in the direction of a standardisation of procedures in the best interests of applicants.

We need to find ways of improving access to the legal system for black women, women living in rural areas, and women with disabilities. This study has been able to do little more than highlight some of the problems and point the way to possible areas for reform. There is a need for research which is specifically geared to the requirements of these particular groups.

Research into the policies and practices of local authority housing departments in regard to domestic violence is also needed, as is further work on the role of the police, particularly in the enforcement of injunctions, undertakings and personal protection orders. Our research indicates an enormous gap between what is in principle available, and what happens in practice. Whether this is the case in other parts of the country has yet to be determined.

Conclusion

Our research has highlighted three main areas of concern. Firstly, there is the legislation itself. The criteria for awarding exclusion orders, and for adding powers of arrest to an injunction or other court order are, in our view, too restrictive. They display excessive concern for the rights of violent men, but often deny women the right of effective and rapid protection from abuse. We also believe that the legislation should be rationalised so that regardless of marital status or living arrangements, any woman could get effective protection from a partner or ex-partner, whether her case is heard in the county or the high court, or before the magistrates.

Secondly, there are problems regarding the procedures and practical arrangements for obtaining protection. We have drawn attention to issues such as inadequate waiting facilities at the courts, formal and intimidating court procedures, lack of appropriate interpreting services, and restricted access to legal advice. These problems are particularly acute for black women, women living in rural areas, those whose first language is not English, women with disabilities, and those who ate ineligible for legal aid.

Thirdly, and underpinning and reinforcing the inadequacies in legislation and procedures, are the attitudes of many of those who advise women or administer the law. Many solicitors, barristers, judges, and police officers are not sufficiently sensitive to the woman's situation. They do not always seem to realise the courage it takes for a woman to seek help from a stranger. Going to court is, for lawyers, a routine matter, but for the woman it is usually her first experience. Many lawyers seem unable to imagine themselves in the woman's position, and their understanding is limited because of their lack of experience and failure of imagination. It is evident from some of the exchanges we have witnessed that "winning" or "losing" cases is, for lawyers, rather like a game — though the results of that "game" may eventually have effect on their careers. For the woman, however, the judgement will have a crucial effect on her future life and happiness.

Particular attention should be paid to the difficulties we have identified in enforcing court orders. Again, this comes back to the attitudes of all those involved. It is useless, for example, for a judge to emphasise in court that the breach of an undertaking is treated as seriously as the breach of an injunction if, in the event, neither the police nor the judge at a future committal hearing seems to demonstrate this seriousness in practice. It is distressing for a woman if the police, on being called to her home, make disparaging or patronising remarks, or if they appear to sympathise with her abuser. It is even worse if they fail to come at all. We have not paid particular attention to police practices in this study, but it is clear from some of the interviews that — in spite of force orders and recommendations — *some* police officers still dismiss "domestic incidents" as irritating but unimportant interruptions to "real" police business.

Whatever legal reforms may be made, and whatever changes may be made to court procedures, without effective enforcement, by police officers and by courts, injunctions and protection orders will continue to be "not worth the paper they're written on".

Footnotes

1. Some judges, informally, allow a woman to take someone else in with her, but this is unusual and may only happen in certain courts (e.g. Middlesbrough).

APPENDIX 1: TABLES

Table 1:
Source of interview sample

Contacted at court	6
Contacted via solicitor	9
Responded to poster	1
Contacted through W.A. refuge	4
Personal contact	11
Total	**31**

Table 2: Marital status of woman in relation to her abuser, at time of abuse

Married	26
Cohabiting	2
Divorced	2
Never lived together	1
Total	**31**

Table 3: Length of time with abuser

Lived together less than a year	4
Lived together between 1 and 3 years inclusive	2
Lived together between 4 and 6 years inclusive	5
Lived together between 7 and 10 years inclusive	9
Lived together between 11 and 19 years inclusive	4
Lived together 20 years and over	3
Never lived together	1
No information	3
	31

Table 4: Ethnic origin of interview sample

	Interviewee	Partner
Asian	11	12
Afro/Caribbean	1	2
White	19	17
Total	**31**	**31**

Table 5: Number of children of women in sample

	Living with woman	Living elsewhere
One child	7	–
2 children	10	3
3 children	8	–
4 or more children	3	–
Has never had children	–	n/a
Total	**28**	**3**

Table 6: Age of youngest child

0 - 4 years	13
5 - 10 years	12
11 - 16 years	3
17 years and over	3
Total	31 women

Table 7: Employment status of sample

	Interviewee	Partner
Emp. full-time/self-employed	3	19
Employed part-time	7	1
Unemployed (signing on)	-	2
Non-employed*	17	2
Student	2	-
Not known	2	7
Total	31	31

* Most of the women and one of the men in this category were caring for children. Two women were chronically sick. One of the men was engaged in illegal activities.

Table 8: Housing situation of interview sample

	When abused	Currently
Tenant, own name	4	7
Tenant, joint names	5	3
Tenant, man's name	1	-
Owner/occupier, own name	2	2
Owner/occupier, joint names	9	6
Owner/occupier, man's name	5	4
Refuge	-	4
Other*	2	2
Not known	3	3
Total	31	31

* house owned by relative

Table 9: Legal measures taken, and results

	Applied for	Received	Breached
County court: non-mol.	19	9 ⎤	8
non-mol. undertaking	–	6 ⎦	
County court: exclusion	13	8 ⎤	2
exclusion undertaking	–	3 ⎦	
(cross undertakings)*	–	(3)	(2)
Magistrates' court: PPO	1	1	–
Magistrates' court: exclusion	1	–	–
Power of arrest attached	3	1	–
Other (i.e. prosecution)	2	2	n/a
None of these	9	n/a	n/a

* All these women had applied for non-molestation orders and/or exclusion orders, and are also included in those figures.

Table 10: Court observations: Number of sessions observed in each court

Bristol county court	(7 different judges) 17
Bristol/Northavon magistrates' courts	2
Kendal county court	1
Kendal magistrates' court	2

Table 11: Court observations: Number of relevant observations

Bristol county court	172
Bristol/Northavon magistrates' courts	3
Kendal county court	1
Kendal magistrates' court	2

Table 12: Cases observed

	Application	Outcome
Personal protection	2	4
Personal protection & exclusion	3	–
Non-molestation injunction	155	88
Ouster/exclusion injunction	110	66
Powers of arrest attached	26	23
Committal for breach	19	3
Undertaking by man	–	54
(cross-undertakings)	–	(14)
Adjourned/withdrawn	–	26

Table 13: Injunctions and other court orders in England and Wales

	Domestic Violence and Matrimonial Proceedings Act, 1976		Ancillary to matrimonial proceedings		Family Protection Orders under the Domestic Proceedings and Magistrates' Courts' Act, 1978		Matrimonial Homes' Act 1983 (1967) s.1	
	No. injuncs.	with p. of a.	No. injuncs.	with p. of a.	No. applics.*	Awarded with p. of A.	In mat. proc.	Not in mat. proc.
1976			12,371		not applicable		Figures not available	
1977	2,393	(774)	13,319	(326)				
1978	6,386	(1,489)	13,176	(683)				
1979	6,794	(1,702)	14,016	(1,049)				
1980	6,399	(1,553)	16,275	(1,404)	Figures not available			
1981	6,809	(1,774)	17,409	(1,300)			65	
1982	7,474	(1,876)	26,428	(1,673)			53	
1983	10,453	(2,501)	15,051**	(1,535)	7,740	(2,020)	1,071	
1984	14,130	(3,568)	12,097**	(1,489)	8,480	(2,090)	1,898	
1985	13,020 (non-mol. 9,202)	(3,314)	3,879***	2,480	6,770	(1,970)	807	239
1986	15,585 (non-mol. 10,826)	(4,005)	3,869	2,797	6,350	(2,030)	600	206
1987	15,984 (non-mol. 11,081)	(4,623)	3,489	2,924	5,760	(1,780)	359	121
1988	18,766 (non-mol. 13,133)	(4,996)	2,549	2,987	5,510	(1,780)	181	72

* Around 60% were granted. (A high proportion of "on notice" applications are withdrawn.)
** Excludes ex parte applications.
*** Injunctions under the Matrimonial Causes Act are not included from 1985, unless a power of arrest is added (next column).

Sources: Judicial Statistics published annually by the Lord Chancellor's Department HMSO.
Statistics of Domestic Proceedings in Magistrates' Courts published annually by the Home Office, HMSO.

APPENDIX 2:

A: Interview Schedule

EXPLAIN OBJECT OF STUDY – mention following points: -

- Who we are.
- Our concern for women who experience violence from men.
- Does the law offer any protection?
- What are the alternatives?
- *Your* experiences.
- If you've used the legal process – what's wrong with it?
- Hope to make recommendations that will make things better for other women.

STRESS CONFIDENTIALITY
EXPAND AS NECESSARY

Point out that we are interested in the WOMAN'S OWN ACCOUNT, and that we would like her to talk about everything that is important to *her,* in her own words (and to interrupt if she wants to.)

N.B. This is a general guide, only. Extra questions may need to be asked for certain groups – e.g. women with disabilities, or black women.

Section I: Introduction and preliminary details

N.B. The assumption is that the woman is or has been living with a violent/abusive man.

In the minority of cases where the partner was never a cohabitee, questions may need to modified slightly.

1. How long have you been (OR, how long were you) living with (violent partner)?

. . . . years

2. *If applicable.*
   (If NO) – When did you stop living with him?

3. Are you married to him?   Yes/No

4. Do you have any children   Yes/No
   How many?
   Ages/Sexes
   Are they all living with you? (Check details).

141

OPTIONAL – HOUSING INFORMATION

In Pilot Study, try this section here, and also try it in Section V.

A. Could I ask you a few questions about the accommodation you are/were living in with X.

(EXPLAIN: This is helpful in getting a full picture of your situation and kinds of steps you might be able to take, to get protections and a secure home of your own).

    Is it a house or a flat? (bedsit, B & B etc.)
    Are/were you buying it or renting it?
    Joint names/his name only/your name only?
    If renting – council? housing association? private landlord?
    Did/do you like the house/flat?
    Do you like the area?

B. Do you want to stay/go back to the same house/same area?
    PROBE as appropriate.

C. *If relevant* – (*i.e.* if she is no longer living in the same accommodation as she shared with man).

Now can I ask you a few questions about the kind of accommodation you're living in now?

    Are you staying with friends/family?
    In B & B?
    In a refuge?
    Other
    How long have you been there?
    Problems with this accommodation?

  5. To ALL women
And would you mind telling me how old you are?

Section II: Background and history of violent relationship

1. *Introduce the next few questions* with something on the following lines, according to the point of contact:

Now as you know, I asked to talk to you because you've just gone to court/consulted a solicitor/gone into a refuge/contacted Women's Aid/consulted CAB .... (etc.) because your husband/partner has been violent or abusive towards you.

I wonder if you could tell me about the most recent incident, that led you to take this step?

PROBE SYMPATHETICALLY as appropriate, in order to learn what led to the decision to take action.

142

2. And can you tell me how all this started? – When did (X) first behave like that towards you?

   Can you tell me about it?

PROBE SYMPATHETICALLY AS NECESSARY
CHECK – was she frightened of him, uneasy, before this?

3. And since then?

PROBE SYMPATHETICALLY AS NECESSARY in order to get a general picture of the extent, frequency and duration of violence; occasions on which violence occurs; whether it has got worse/more frequent over time – or the reverse; whether it is associated with alcohol or drug use/unemployment/stress at work or home/etc.

4. And what do *you* usually do when he does that kind of thing?

PROBE AS APPROPRIATE
CHECK – intervention from others? – *e.g.* neighbours? children?

5. *(If relevant)* Has he ever been violent to the children, or abused them in any way.

6. Have you ever – left home/consulted a solicitor/taken him to court/called the police/gone to Social Services/contacted Women's Aid – (before this?)

Ask FIRST about previous attempts to do the same as she has done this time. THEN go on to ask:

   Have you ever taken any other action? – for example, have you:
   Left home?
   Consulted a solicitor?
   Taken your partner to court?
   Called the police?
   Gone to Social Services?
   Contacted Women's Aid?
   Anything else?

Ask about ALL that may be relevant: in each case, ACTION taken, WHY, and OUTCOME.

NOW GO TO SECTION III if woman IS APPLYING for a court order
SECTION IV if she is NOT applying for a court order.

Section III: For women who ARE APPLYING for a court order

Others go to Section IV.

N.B. Wording of questions may need to be changed appropriately, according to whether woman is in the process of applying for or has recently achieved, her injunction. I am assuming here that she will be interviewed very shortly after the successful?) court hearing.

1. When did you first realise you could go to court to get protection from your violent partner?

CHECK – knowledge of injunctions?
PROBE – how did she learn?
    e.g. From solicitor/law centre?
    Friend/neighbour/colleague at work?
    Relative?
    Women's Aid – local group?
    WAFE – National Helpline?
    Social worker?
    Police?
    Housing department?
    CAB?
    Read about it – leaflet, newspaper/magazine, other?
    Other source of information?

2. Were you clear what you were going for?

3. Did you decide to get an injunction straight away (*i.e.* immediately after learning that you could).

PROBE – why/why not?
Did you consider alternative courses of action?
PROBE – what?

4. Has your solicitor been helpful?

PROBE – has s/he outlined the various options available?
CHECK – which?
Did s/he mention you could:
    get non-molestation/personal protection order?
    get him out of the house (ouster/exclusion order)?
    ask for police powers of arrest to be attached to the injunction?
    get an injunction *without* going for divorce at the same time?
    use either magistrates or county court?
    not go for an injunction at all, but approach Homeless Persons Department of the Council for re-housing?
    go into a refuge?
or did s/he simply advise one course of action?
Did s/he tell you why s/he recommended that?
Does s/he give you time to talk things over?
Does s/he listen sympathetically?
Did s/he put you in touch with other sources of help/advice – *e.g.* Women's Aid?

5. How did you come to choose this particular solicitor?
   PROBE as appropriate for degree of knowledge/access/chance/choice.

6. Did you have any difficulty in understanding the things your solicitor was telling you?
If appropriate
   language difficulties?
   interpreter offered?

7. Once you decided to go for an injunction, how long did it take?
   Did you go for an emergency injunction? (called *ex parte*).
   Any problems getting legal aid? – emergency legal aid?

8. Is this the first time you have gone for an injunction?
   If not, PROBE what happened last time, as appropriate.

9. What kind of injunction have you got? (are you going for?)
   PROBE – non-molestation/exclusion
   which court? – (magistrates/county court)
   which Act? – (DVA/DPMCA/Matrimonial causes/other)
   PROBE perceived advantages/disadvantages
   powers of arrest?
   how long is it for?

10. Is that what you/your solicitor asked for?
    PROBE – any difference?
    'undertaking' instead of injunction – how does she feel about that?
    What kind of evidence did you have to give? – *e.g.* witnesses; medical evidence; photographs; etc.

8. Do you expect your partner will keep to the terms of the injunctions?
   PROBE – why/why not?
   What she might do about it.

11. Are you taking any other proceedings against him at present?
    PROBE – criminal prosecution (who initiated this?)
    divorce/separation?
    custody/maintenance, etc.

12. What did you feel about the process of going to court?
    outside court?
    inside court?
    adjournments?
    custody/access arrangements?

13. Did you leave home at all while you were waiting for the case to come to court?

PROBE AS APPROPRIATE – why/why not?
where did you go
did you take the children with you? (If not, why? Where did they go?)
are you still there?
have you gone home now? – why/why not?
future plans – *e.g.* re. re-housing, etc.

If did NOT leave home. Did you do anything else to protect yourself while you were waiting for the injunction to go through?

14. *(If not already covered)*
What do you hope to achieve by having an injunction?

15. Have you consulted any other agencies for advice or support?
e.g. Women's Aid
Social Services
Housing Department
Police
PROBE for perceived helpfulness of each one.

If police involved – did they ever suggest/initiate prosecution of your partner for this incident?

16. Anything else you would like to say?

GO TO SECTION V.

Section IV: For women NOT applying for court order

1. Did you know you could go to court to get protection from your violent partner?
PROBE – extent of knowledge – injunctions?
– kinds of injunctions? (non-molestation, exclusion, powers of arrest, etc.)
length of time known
how did she learn?
Have you ever asked anyone for advice? – *e.g.*

solicitor/law centre?
friend/relative/neighbour/colleague at work?
Women's Aid – local group?
Women's Aid – national helpline?
Social worker?
Police?
housing department?
CAB?
Other?

146

2. Have you *ever* obtained a court order to protect you?

   If YES – were you clear what you were going for?
   What happened?

   PROBE as appropriate.

3. *(If knows about injunctions, and/or has used them before)*
   Why did you decide *not* to go for an injunction this time?

   PROBE as appropriate.

4. *(if not already known)*
   Do you have a solicitor?

5. *Then, if relevant*
   How did you come to choose this particular solicitor?

   PROBE as appropriate for degree of knowledge/access/chance/choice.

6. Has your solicitor been helpful?

   PROBE AS APPROPRIATE – *e.g.* did s/he outline the various options
   available?
   CHECK which – *e.g.* divorce
   injunctions
   custody, access, maintenance
   options regarding rehousing
   go into refuge

   Or did s/he tell you what you should do? or advice a particular course
   of action?

   If YES – did s/he tell you why s/he recommended that?
   Did s/he give you time to talk things over?
   Listen sympathetically?
   Put you in touch with other sources of help? – (which?)

7. Did you have any difficulty in understanding the things your solicitor
   was telling you?

   If appropriate – language difficulties?
   interpreter offered?

8. Are you taking legal proceedings of any kind at present?
   e.g. divorce/separation
   custody
   maintenance
   criminal prosecution of partner (who initiated this?)

9. *If YES* and she has already been to court:
   What did you think of the process of going to court?

outside court?
inside court?
adjournments?
custody/access arrangements?

10. What (other) agencies have you consulted?
    e.g. Women's Aid
    Social Services
    Housing Department
    police

PROBE for perceived helpfulness of each one.

If police involved – did they ever suggest/initiate prosecution of your partner for this incident?

PROBE as appropriate.

11. What are you hoping to do now? (*e.g.* go for divorce, get re-housed, go back home, etc.)

12. Anything else you would like to say?

NOW GO TO SECTION V.

Section V: For ALL women: Factual Details

N.B. You may not need to ask all these questions, as the points might have already emerged in earlier discussion. If in doubt, check information.

EXPLAIN why we would like to know these things – *i.e.* that their experiences, and the options available to them may vary according to their employment and financial situation and their housing status.

1. Do you have a job at present?
   nature of work
   full-time/part-time
   how long have you been doing that?

2. *If living apart from partner, and HAS a job*
   Do you earn enough to live on?
   If NO what are you doing for money at present?
   PROBE AS APPROPRIATE

3. *(If no job now)*
   What was the last job you had?
   Why did you give it up?

   Check whether any connection with violent incident – *e.g.* moving into refuge.

   Would you like another job now?

If YES – is there anything preventing you?
PROBE as appropriate.
CHECK with all women: (other) disabilities?

5. *To those with no job and living apart from partner*
What are you doing for money at present?
Any problems managing?

6. *To ALL women*
Does your husband/partner have a job?
nature of work
permanent/casual
how long has he been doing it?
spells of unemployment

If NOT asked in Section I:
7 Now I'd like to ask you a few questions about the accommodation you are/were living in with X.

Is it a house or a flat? (or bedsit, B & B, etc.)
are/were you buying it or renting it?
joint names/his name only/your name only/other

If renting – council/housing association/private landlord

8. Did/do you like the house/flat?
Did you like the area?

9. *If relevant*
Do you want to go back to the same place/stay in the same area?

10. *If relevant* – (*i.e.* if she is no longer living in the same accommodation as she shared with the man):

Now can I ask you a few questions about the kind of accommodation you're living in now?
Are you staying with friends/family?
in B & B?
in a refuge?
other?
How long have you been there?
Problems with this accommodation?

11. *To ALL women*
EXPLAIN why we are asking this question:
Concerned that the system should be fair and work well for *all* women. Black and ethnic minority women might be treated differently, or have particular difficulties. In some cases, language difficulties.

Would you mind telling me how you would describe your ethnic group?

After self-definition, SHOW CARD.

Which of the following best describes your ethnic origin?
And your partner?
ASIAN – Bangladeshi
British
Chinese
Indian
Pakistani
other Asian
BLACK – African
Afro-Caribbean/West Indian
British
Guyanese
other Black
WHITE – British
Irish
other European

13. *If appropriate*
At any stage do you feel that you have been treated differently because of your colour/ethnic origin?

14. *Summarise* – So far you've told me . . . .
Is there anything else you'd like to say?

THANK HER FOR HER HELP.

EXPLAIN THAT WE WOULD LIKE TO DO ONE OR MORE FOLLOW-UP INTERVIEWS, to see how things are going.

Ask if that would be all right, how to get in touch with her etc.

LEAVE CARD with her, so she can change agreement if necessary – or in case she can't or is reluctant to give an address.

ALSO, leave sheet of LOCAL CONTACT NUMBERS for advice, support, etc.

B: Question Guide for Solicitors

1. How often are you consulted by women who want advice regarding domestic violence?
   How soon would you normally be able to see her?
2. How would you reassure a client?
   How much do you explain to her? e.g. about the procedure, or the options available.
   Do you give *her* the choice of what to do?
3. What would you normally advise? e.g.
   injunction in county court?
   personal protection order in magistrates' court?
   go straight for divorce (if relevant)?
   Why?
4. Do you have an emergency contact number for evenings/weekends? (or is there one available via police, social services, etc?)
   What would you advise a woman to do if she was beaten up on a Friday night or a Saturday night, or just before a Bank Holiday?
5. Under what circumstances would you go for an *ex parte* injunction?/protection order?
6. Would there be any difficulties in getting emergency legal aid for an *ex parte* application?
   How soon could you get it?
7. How soon could you normally get non-emergency legal aid?
   Would this ever hold up an application? Under what circumstances?
8. Are non-molestation orders without ousters, when the woman stays at home, ever any use?
   In what circumstances would you try this? (e.g. as an interim measure in case of divorce? if woman wished relationship to continue but simply wished to show him she was serious about ending violence?)
9. If a woman is married, would you tend to advise her to go straight for a divorce, and get the injunction ancillary to that?
   Why/why not?
10. If a woman is not eligible for legal aid, how much would it cost her to go for an injunction?
    Is it cheaper under some legislation (e.g. DVA; or DPMCA) than others?
    If she is *not* living with the man, and therefore has to apply in a civil damages/trespass action, is this more expensive? more complicated? Why/how?
11. Sometimes there is a reference in court to "all the paperwork" needed in injunction applications.

Is it excessive?

Could it be simplified? How?

Is this an advantage in using magistrates' courts? — or does that lead to other difficulties do you think?

12. Under what circumstances would you use a barrister for an injunction application?

13. In your experience, in this area, are injunctions (in the county court) available in cases of mental/emotional abuse?

What criteria would be used (e.g. effects on children). Have you noticed any change in the availability of injunctions in such cases, over the years you have been practising?

14. How important is it that injunctions and committal notices are exactly in the prescribed form?

Are there any problems here?

15. (Cumbria only) Do you find there are any special considerations or difficulties, practising in a rural area? e.g.

availability of courts?

difficulties for women travelling to court or to solicitor's office?

nowhere for them to go while waiting for case to be heard? etc.

16. What proportion of black women do you see for injunctions/domestic violence advice?

Do you feel the legislation is under-used by black women and ethnic minorities generally?

Are there any special needs or problems here, in increasing the availability/suitability for black and ethnic minority women?

17. What considerations govern your choice between county courts and magistrates' courts for this type of work?

18. Are there any special considerations if a woman has disabilities?

If the man has disabilities? (for example the house may be specially designed for the disabled partner; there may be problems of communication, access to solicitor's office or courts, etc.)

19. Have you ever had any problems in obtaining powers of arrest, when you feel these are justified?

Do you think powers of arrest are attached often enough?

20. Committals: why the reluctance to commit until orders have been repeatedly breached?

Is this justified?

21. How do you feel about undertakings?

Do you think women are put under pressure to accept an undertaking when the man offers one? Is this justifiable?

What about cross undertakings — where the woman also has to promise not to molest, etc.:

Does this tend to happen much here?

How do you feel about it?

22. (Bristol only) Injunctions are mostly held on Fridays and the court is set up for this purpose.

What are the advantages and disadvantages of this?

Is this specific to Bristol or does it happen in other areas, as far as you know?

23. Any other points / problems regarding injunctions / personal protection orders?

24. How useful do you think court welfare officers can be in cases of domestic violence?

25. Do you have a conciliation service here?

(If so) What do you feel about it, in cases of domestic violence.

26. In your experience, do most injunctions and personal protection orders have the desired effect?

27. How about the facilities of the court? — the waiting room, etc. Suggestions for improvements?

28. Is there any way, do you think, of making the whole process of going to court less stressful?

APPENDIX 3: CONTACT LETTER

Women's
Aid
Federation
England ltd

Bristol Polytechnic

Coldharbour Lane, Frenchay
Bristol BS16 1QY
Telephone: (0272) 656261 Ext 2364
Director A C Morris MA FCA FSS FRSA

Dear

I know this is not the best of times to approach you, but I would very much appreciate your help.

I am looking at the effectiveness of the law protecting women and children who experience violence from within the home, and I would like to talk to a number of women who, like yourself, have a violent husband or partner, and are thinking about what course of action to take.

I have worked for women in Bristol for several years and I have some idea of the problems you face. Some people believe that going to court to get protection from a violent man is the solution, but it does not always work out like that. Perhaps the law could be improved; or perhaps legal proceedings are not the answer at all. I want to know what *you* think about this.

If you think you could spare the time to talk to me, I would be very grateful if you could 'phone me or fill in the slip below and either post it in the enclosed envelope, or give it to your solicitor who will pass it on to me. I have an office at Bristol Polytechnic but also work from home and could meet you at either place, or at your home, or anywhere else you would like to suggest.

Of course I am very concerned not to add in any way to the risks you face. I will treat any information you give me as completely confidential, and will not give anyone your name and address, without asking you first. (You can use another name if you like, and you need not give me your address.) I will not, of course, use true names in my report.

I would be very grateful if you agreed to see me.

Anjali Gupta.

Anjali Gupta

Jackie Barron

I would like to help with your research.

Name . . . .

You can contact me at . . . .

. . . .

Please do NOT call at the following times . . . .

BIBLIOGRAPHY

Acker. S., Barry, K., and Esseveld. J. (1983) "Objectivity and truth: problems in doing feminist research" *Women's Studies International Forum* 6 (4) (pp.423-435).

Ahmed, Shama (1986) "Cultural racism in work with Asian women and girls" in Ahmed, S., Cheetham, J., and Small, J. *Social Work with Black Children and their Families* (London: Batsford).

Alibhai, Yasmin (1989) "For better or for worse" *New Statesman and Society* January 6th 1989 (pp.22-23).

Amos, Valerie and Parmar, Pratibha (1984) "Challenging imperialist feminism" *Feminist Review* 17 (pp.3-20).

Atkins, Susan and Hoggatt, Brenda (1984) *Women and the Law* (Oxford: Blackwell).

Bainham, Andrew (1980) "Conduct and exclusion orders" *Family Law* 10 (pp.228-230).

Bangham, L. (1986) "Domestic violence: Too late to mediate" *Police Chief* 53 (June 1986).

Bard, Morton and Berkowitz, B. (1969) "Family disturbances as a police function" in Cohn, S. (ed.) *Law Enforcement Science and Technology II* (Chicago: ITT Research Institute).

Bard, Morton and Zacker, J. (1971) "Prevention of family violence: Dilemmas of police intervention" *Journal of Marriage and the Family* 33 (54) (pp.671-682).

Baron, Ava (1987) "Feminist legal strategies: The powers of difference" in Hess, Beth B. and Ferree, Myra Marx *Analysing Gender* (Newbury Park: Sage).

Bates, Frank (1981) "A plea for the battered husband" *Family Law* Vol. 11 (pp.90-92).

Bauer, Carol and Ritt, Lawrence (1983) "A husband is a beating animal" *International Journal of Women's Studies* 6 (2) (pp.99-118).

Bell, Daniel (1985) "A multi-year study of Ohio urban, suburban and rural police depositions of domestic disputes" *Victimology* Vol.10 (pp.301-310).

Berk, R. and Newton, P.J. (1985) "Does arrest really deter wife battery? An effort to replicate the findings of the Minneapolis spouse abuse experiment" *American Sociological Review* 50 (pp.253-62).

Berk, R. and others (1984) "Cops on call: Summoning the police to the scene of spousal violence" *Law Society Review* 18, No. 3 (pp.479-498).

Berkowitz, Bernard (1980) "Towards a reappraisal of family law ideology" *Family Law* 10 (pp.164-172).

Binney, V., Harknell, G., and Nixon, J. (1981) *Leaving Violent Men* (WAFE).

"Black women organising autonomously" *Feminist Review* 17 (1984) (pp.83-89)

Blair, S. (1979) "Making the legal system work for battered women" in Moore, D. M. (ed.) *Battered Women* (Beverly Hills: Sage).

Bograd, Michele (1988) "How battered women and abusive men account for domestic violence: Excuses, justifications or explanations? in Hotaling *et al.* (ed.).

Borkowski, Margaret, Murch, Mervyn, and Walker, V. (1983) *Marital Violence: The Community Response* (Tavistock).

Bottomley, Anne (1985) "What is happening to family law? A feminist critique of conciliation" in Brophy, J. and Smart, C. (ed.) *Women in Law* (London: RKP).

Bourlet, Alan Robert (1988) *Police intervention in marital violence* Univ. of Kent M.Phil Dissertation).

Bozzi, V. (1986) "Arrest deters batterers" *Psychology Today* 20 (p.8).

Brannen, Julia (1988) "The study of sensitive subjects: A note on interviewing" *Sociological Review* Vol.36, No. 3 (pp.552-563).

Breines, W. and Gordon, L. (1984) "The new scholarship on family violence" *Signs* 8 (pp.490-531).

Brophy, J. and Smart, C. (1981) "From disregard to disrepute: The position of women in family law" *Feminist Review* 9 (pp.3-16).

Brophy, Julia and Smart, Carol (1985) *Women-in-Law* (London: RKP).

Buzawa, Eve (1988) "Explaining variations in police response to domestic violence: A case study in Detroit and New England" in Hotaling *et al.* (ed.).

Cain, M. (1986) "Realism, feminism, methodology and the law" *International Journal of Sociology of Law* 14 (pp.255-267).

Cameron, Jeremy (1988) "Violent men: The only remedy" *Social Work Today* Vol. 19, No. 29 (p.25).

Carlson, Bonnie (1977) "Battered women and their assailants" *Social Work* 22 (6) (pp.455-460).

Cavanagh, Catherine (1978) *Battered women and social control: A study of the help-seeking behaviour of battered women and the help-giving behaviour of those from whom they seek help* (Unpublished M.A. thesis, Univ. of Stirling).

Chesler, Phyllis (1986) *Mothers on Trial* (New York: McGraw Hill).

Chester, R. and Strether, J. (1972) "Cruelty in English divorce: Some empirical findings" *Journal of Marriage and the Family* 34 (pp.706-712).

Coleman, C. and Bottomley, K. (1976) "Police conceptions of 'crime' and 'no crime' " *Criminal Law Review* Vol.5, No. 2 (pp.344-360).

Coley, S. M. and Beckett, J. O. (1988) "Black battered women: A review of the empirical literature" *Journal of Counselling and Development* Vol. 66, No. 6 (pp.266-270).

Crites, Laura (1987) "Wife abuse: The judicial record" in Crites and Hepperle (*op. cit.*).

Crites, Laura and Hepperle, Winifred (1987) *Women, the Courts and Equality* Beverly Hills: Sage) (refers to USA).

Davis, Gwyn and Bader, Kay (1985) "In court mediation: The consumer view" *Family Law* Vol. 15 (pp.42-49 and 82-86).

Davis, Gwyn and Roberts, Marian (1988) *Access to Agreement* (Open University Press).

Davis, Gwyn and Roberts Marian (1989) "Mediation and the battle of the sexes" *Family Law* Vol.19 (pp.305-306).

Davis, L. W. (1987) "Battered women: The transformation of a social problem" *Social Work* 32 (pp.307-311).

Delamont, Sara and Ellis, Rhian (1979) *Statutory and Voluntary Responses to Domestic Violence in Wales* (SRU Working Paper No. 6, University College, Cardiff).

Dobash, R., and Dobash, R., (1980) *Violence against Wives* (Open Books).

Dobash, Russell P. and Dobash, R. Emerson (1987) "The context specific approach" in Finkelhor *et. al.* (ed.) *The Dark Side of Families* (Beverly Hills: Sage).

Domestic Violence Prevention Project: Panel discussion *Police Chief* March 1987.

Donato, K. and Bowker, L. (1984) "Understanding the help-seeking behaviour of battered women: A comparison of traditional social service agencies and women's groups" *International Journal of Women's Studies* (7) (pp.99-109).

Eaton, Mary (1986) *Justice for Women? Family, Courts and Social Control* (Open Univ. Press).

Edwards, Anne (1987) "Male violence in feminist theory: An analysis of the changing conceptions of sex/gender violence and male dominance" in Hanmer, J. and Maynard, M. (ed.) *Women and Social Control* (London: Macmillan).

Edwards, Susan (1985a) "Compelling a reluctant spouse: Policing the prosecution process" *New Law Journal* Vol. 135 (pp.1076-1078).

Edwards, Susan (1985b) *Gender, Sex and the Law* (London: Croom Helm).

Edwards, Susan (1985c) "A sociolegal evaluation of gender ideologies in domestic violence assault and spousal homicides" *Victimology* 10 (pp.186-205).

Edwards, Susan (1986a) "Police attitudes and dispositions in domestic disputes: The London study" *Police Journal* July 1986 (pp.230-241).

Edwards, Susan (1986b) *The Police Response to Domestic Violence in London* (Polytechnic of Central London).

Edwards, Susan (1986c) "The real risks of violence behind closed doors" *New Law Journal* Vol. 136, No. 6284 (pp.1191-3).

Edwards, Susan (1987) "Provoking her own demise: From common assault to homicide" in Hanmer and Maynard (ed.) (*op. cit.*).

Edwards, Susan (1989a) "Policing 'domestic violence' ". Paper presented at British Sociological Association Annual Conference, March 1989, Plymouth Polytechnic.

Edwards, Susan (1989b) *Policing "Domestic" Violence* (London: Sage).

Edwards, Susan and Halpern, Ann (1988) "Conflicting interests: protecting children or protecting title to property" *Journal of Social Welfare Law* Vol. 10, No. 2 (pp.110-124).

Ellis, Rhian (1983) "Family pastoral, family violence: Battered women in rural areas" (Paper presented at BSA Conference, Cardiff, April 1983).

Erez, Edna (1986) "Intimacy, violence and the police" *Human Relations* 39 (March 1986) (USA).

Faragher, Tony (1985) "The police response to violence against women in the home" in Pahl (ed.) *Private Violence and Public Policy.*

Ferguson, H. (1987) "Mandating arrests for domestic violence" *FBI Law Enforcement Bulletin* (56) (p.6-11).

Ferraro, Kathleen (1989a) "The legal response to woman battering in the United Staters" in Hanmer, Radford and Stanko (ed.) *Women, Policing and Male Violence* (Routledge).

Ferraro, Kathleen (1989b) "Policing woman battering" *Social Problems* Vol. 36, No. 1 (pp.61-74).

Field, Martha and Field, Henry (1973) "Marital violence and the criminal process" *Social Services Review* 47 (pp.221).

Finch, Janet (1983) "It's great to have someone to talk to: The ethics and politics of interviewing women" in Bell, Colin and Roberts, Helen (ed.) *Social Researching* (London: RKP).

Finer Committee (1974) *Report of the Committee on One Parent Families* (London: HMSO).

Finkelhor, David et. al. (ed.) *The Dark Side of Families: Current Family Violence Research* (Beverly Hills: Sage).

Finn, Peter (1989) "Statutory authority in the use and enforcement of civil protection orders against domestic abuse" *Family Law Quarterly* Vol. XXIII No. 1 (pp.43-73).

Foakes, Joane (1984) *Family Violence: Law and Practice* (Hemstal Press).

Ford, David A. (1983) "Wife beating and criminal justice: A study of victim decision-making" *"Family Relations* 32 (4) (pp.463-475).

Franzway, Suzanne, Court, Daine, Connell, R.W. (1989) *Staking a Claim: Feminism, Bureaucracy and the State* (London: Polity).

Freeman, M.D.A. (1987) *Dealing with Domestic Violence* (CCH Editions).

Freeman, M.D.A. (ed.) (1984) *The State, the Law and the Family* (Tavistock).

Fricker, Nigel (1988a) "Committal for contempt in the county court" Family Law Vol. 8 (pp.232-253).

Fricker, Nigel (1988b) "Specimen forms for anti-molestations injunctions and exclusion orders" *Family Law* Vol. 18 (pp.345-349).

Gardner, Paul (1987) *Emergency Family Remedies* (London: Longman Practice Notes) (1st ed.).

Gelles, Richard (1972) *The Violent Home* (Beverly Hills: Sage).

Gelles, Richard and Cornell, Claire Pedrick (1985) *Intimate Violence in Families* (Beverly Hills: Sage).

Gelles, R.J. and Maynard, P.E (1987) "A structural family systems approach to intervention in cases of family violence" *Family Relations* 36.

Gerhardt, V. (1979) "Coping and social action" *Sociology of Health and Illness* 1 (2) (pp.212-230).

Gondolf, Edward (1988) *Battered Women as Survivors* (Lexington, Mass.: Lexington Books).

Graham, Hilary (1984) "Do her answers fit his questions?" in Garmarnikow, E. et. al. (ed.) *The Public and the Private* (London: Heinemann).

Grau, Janice, Fagan, Jeffrey, Wexler, Sandra (1985) "Restraining orders for battered women: Issues of access and efficacy" *Women and Politics* Vol. 4 (3) (pp.13-28).

Greenblat, C.J. (1985) " 'Don't beat your wife . . . unless': Preliminary findings on normative support for use of physical violence by husbands" *Victimology* 10 (pp.221-241).

Griffiths, A. (1981) "Some battered women in Wales: An interactionist view of their legal problems" *Family Law* Vol. 11 (pp.25-29).

Guru, Surinder (1986) "An Asian women's refuge" in Ahmed, S., Cheetham, J., and Small, J. (ed.) *Social Work with Black Children and their Families* (London: Batsford).

Hamilton, Roger (1984) "Has the House of Lords abolished the Domestic Violence Act for married women?" *Legal Action* March 1984 (pp.25-27)

Hanmer, Jalna and Saunders, Sheila (1984) *Well-founded Fear: A Community Study of Violence to Women* (London: Hutchinson).

Hanmer, Jalna and Stanko, Elizabeth (1985) "Stripping away the rhetoric of protection: Violence to women, law and the state in Britain and the USA" *International Journal of Sociology of Law* 13 (pp.357-374).

Hanmer, Jalna, Radford, Jill and Stanko, Elizabeth A. (ed.) (1989a) *Women, Policing and Male Violence: International Perspectives* (London: Routledge).

Hanmer, J., Radford, J. and Stanko, E. (1989b) "Improving policing for women: The way forward" in Hanmer, Radford, Stanko (ed.) (*op. cit.*).

Harris, R.N. and Bologh, R.W. (1985) "The dark side of love: Blue and white collar abuse" *Victimology* 10 (pp.242-252).

Hoff, Lee Ann (1988) "Collaborative feminist research and the myth of objectivity" in Yllo, Kersti and Bograd, Michele (ed.) *Feminist Perspectives on Wife Abuse* (Beverly Hills: Sage Focus Editions Vol. 93).

Hoggett, B. and Pearl, D. (1987) *The Family, Law and Society: Cases and Materials* (London: Butterworth).

Homer, M., Leonard P. and Taylor, P. (1984) *Private Violence and Public Shame* (Cleveland Refuge and Aid for Women and Children).

Horley, Sandra (1985) "Fall out in the refuges" *New Society* 28/6/85. (pp.488-489).

Horley, Sandra (1988) "Pioneering police plan to help battered women" *Social Work Today* Vol. 19, No. 29 24/3/88.

Hotaling, Gerald, Finkelhor, David, Kirkpatrick, John and Strauss, Murray (ed.) (1988) *Coping with Family Violence: Research and Policy Perspectives* Beverly Hills: Sage).

Hotaling, G., Finkelhor, D., Kirkpatrick, J., and Strauss, M. (1988b) (ed.) *Family Abuse and its Consequences: New Directions in Research* (Newbury Park: Sage).

Hough and Mayhew, M. (1985) *Taking Account of Crime: The Findings from the 1984 British Crime Survey* (London: HMSO).

Humphreys, Janice and Humphreys, William (1985) "Mandatory arrest: A means of primary and secondary prevention of abuse of female partners" *Victimology* Vol. 10 (pp.267-280).

Jesperson, Annelise (1987) "The 'domestics' dilemma" *Police Review* 3/7/87 (pp.1328-9).

Johnson, Norman (ed.) (1985) *Marital Violence* (London: RKP).

Jolin, A. (1983) "Domestic violence legislation: An impact assessment" *Journal of Police Science and Administration* No. 11 (pp.451-6).

Jolly, H. (1985) *Book of Child Care: Complete Guide for Today's Parents* 4th ed. (Allen and Unwin).

Kalmuss, D., and Seltzer, J. A. (1986) "Continuity of marital behaviour in re-marriage: The case of spouse abuse" *Journal of Marriage and the Family* 48 (pp.113-120).

Kantor, G. and Strauss, M. (1987) "The drunken bum theory of wife-beating" *Social Problems* 34 (pp.213-230).

Karpf, Anna (1985) "What turns a man into Mr. Punch? *Guardian* 14/8/85.

Kelly, Liz (1988) *Surviving Sexual Violence* (Cambridge: Polity Press).

159

Kelly, L. and Radford, J. (1987) "The problem of men: Feminist perspectives in sexual violence" in Scraton, P. (ed.) *Law, Order and the Authoritarian State* (Milton Keynes: Open University Press).

Law Commission (1989) *Domestic Violence and the Occupation of the Family Home* Working Paper 113 (London: HMSO).

Leach, Penelope (1988) *Baby and Child* (London: Michael Joseph).

Lees, Sue (1989) "Naggers, whores and libbers: Provoking men to murder" Paper presented at British Sociological Association Annual Conference, Plymouth Polytechnic, March 1989.

Leonard, P., and McLeod, E. (1980) *Marital Violence: Social Construction and Social Service Response* (Department of Applied Social Studies, University of Warwick).

Lockhart, L. (1987) "Re-examination of the effects of race and class on the incidence of marital violence: A search for reliable differences" *Journal of Marriage and the Family* 49 (pp.603–610).

London Strategic Policy Unit (1986) *Police Response to Domestic Violence* (Police Monitoring and Research Group Briefing Paper No. 1 LSPU).

Macauley, Sean (1985) "A wife is not a thump object" *Observer* 15/12/85 (Police and Criminal Evidence Act).

McCann, Kathy (1983) *The Legal Response to Wife Abuse: A Study of Sexist Bias* (Unpublished M.Phil. Thesis, Univ. of Sheffield. Department of Sociolegal Studies).

McCann, Kathryn (1985) "Battered women and the law: The limits of legislation" in Brophy and Smart *op. cit.*

McCann, Kathy, Brown, Pat, and Blandy, Sarah (n.d.) "The monitoring of the Domestic Proceedings and Magistrates' Courts' Act, 1978 (Sheffield Women's Aid).

McEwan, Vera G. (1983) "Jurisdictional defects" *Family Law* 13 (pp.187–188).

McGibbon, Alison, Cooper, Libby and Kelly, Liz (1989) *What Support?* Hammersmith and Fulham Council Community Police Committee Domestic Violence Project. (Polytechnic of North London).

McGregor, O. (1957) *Divorce in England: A Centenary Study* (London: Heinemann).

McGregor, O.R., Blom-Cooper L., and Gibson, C. (1971) *Separated Spouses* (London: Duckworth).

McGuire, Sarah (1988) " 'Sorry, love': Violence against women in the home and the state response" *Critical Social Policy* 23.

McLeod, L. (1983) "Victim non-co-operation in domestic disputes" *Criminology* 21 (p.395).

McNeely, R.L. and Robinson, Gloria (1987) "The truth about domestic violence: A falsely framed issue" *Social Work* Nov–Dec. 87, Vol. 32 No. 6 (pp.485–488).

Maidment, Susan (1977a) "Laws for battered women: Are they an improvement? *Family Law* 7 (pp.50–52).

Maidment, Susan (1977b) "The law's response to marital violence in England and USA" *International Comparative Law Quarterly* 26 (pp.403–444).

Maidment, Susan (1980) "The relevance of criminal law to domestic violence" *Journal of Social Welfare Law* 2 (pp.26–32).

Maidment, S. (1983) "Civil versus criminal: The use of legal remedies in responses to domestic violence in England and Wales" *Victimology* Vol. 8 (pp. 172-187).

Maidment, Susan (1985) "Domestic violence and the law: The 1976 Act and its aftermath" in Johnson (ed.) (*op. cit.*).

Mama, Amina (1989) *The Hidden Struggle: Statutory and Voluntary Sector Responses to Violence against Black women in the Home* (London Race and Housing Research Unit).

Manchester Police Monitoring Unit (1987) *Breaking the Silence: Manchester Women Speak Out* (Manchester City Council).

Marsden, D. (1978) "Sociological perspectives on family violence" in Martin, J.P. (ed.) *Violence in the Family* (London: Wiley).

Marsden, D. and Owens, D. (1975) "Jekyll and Hyde marriages" *New Society* 8/5/75 (p.333).

Martin, J.P. (1978) (ed.) *Violence in the Family* (Chichester: Wiley).

Meredith, E. (1979) "Some possibilities in the proceedings used in cases of abuse in the family" in Hanmer, J. (ed.) *Battered Women and Abused Children* (Occasional Paper No. 4, University of Bradford).

Metropolitan Police Working Party into Marital Violence (1986) Draft Report.

Migdal, S. (1979) "Domestic violence: Has the Act beaten it?" *Family Law* 9 (pp.136-138).

Moore, D.M. (ed.) (1979) *Battered Women* (Beverly Hills: Sage).

Morash, M. (1986) "Wife Battering" *Criminal Justice Abstracts* June 1986 (pp.252-271).

Murch, Mervyn (1981) *The Community Response to Marital Violence* (Department of Social Administration, University of Bristol).

Murch, Mervyn, Borkowski, Margaret, Copner, Rosalie, and Griew, Kathleen (1987) *The Overlapping Family Jurisdiction of Magistrates' Courts and County Courts* (Socio-Legal Centre for Family Studies, Univ. of Bristol).

Myers, M. and Halpern, J. (1979) "Public and Private Trouble" *Social Problems* 26 (4) (p.439).

Newham, London Borough of (1988) "Strategy to Combat Domestic Violence" (Women's Equality Unit and Community Safety Unit, Newham Borough Council, London).

NWAF (1980) *The Domestic Violence Act: How it works in practice.*

Okun, Lewis (1988) "Termination or resumption of cohabitation in woman battering relationships: A statistical study" in Hotaling *et. al.*

Pahl, Jan (1982) "Police response to battered women" *Journal of Social Welfare Law* Vol. 4 (pp.337-343).

Pahl, Jan (ed.) (1985) *Private Violence and Public Policy* (RKP).

Pahl, Jan (1989) *Money and Marriage* (London: Macmillan).

Pahl, Jan (1990) "Household spending, personal spending and the control of money in marriage" *Sociology* Vol. 24 No. 1.

Parker, S. J. (1979) "The taking of recognisances as a matrimonial remedy" *Family Law* 9 (pp.76-78).

Parker, Stephen (1985) "The legal background" in Pahl (ed.) (*op. cit.*).

Parkinson, Patrick (1986) "The Domestic Violence Act and Richards versus Richards" *Family Law* 16 (pp.70-73).

Parmar, Pratibha (1982) "Gender, race and class: Asian women in resistance" in Centre for Contemporary Cultural Studies (ed.) *The Empire Strikes Back: Race and Racism in Britain* (London: Hutchinson).

Parnas, R. (1971) "Police discretion and diversion of incidents of family violence" *Law and Contemporary Problems* 36 (pp.539-564).

Parsloe, S. (1987) "Battered by men and bruised by the law" *Law Magazine* 4/9/87.

Patterson, E.J. (1979) "How the law responds to battered women" in Moore, D.M. (ed.) *op. cit.*

Pattullo, P. (1983) *Judging Women* (London: NCCL, Rights of Women Unit).

Pearl, D. (1986) "Public housing allocation and domestic disputes" in Freeman, M.D.A. (ed.) *Essays in Family Law 1985: Current Legal Problems* (London: Sweet and Maxwell).

Pence, Ellen and Shepard, Melanie (1988) "Integrating theory and practice: The challenge of the battered women's movement" in Yllo and Bograd (ed.) *Feminist Perspectives on Wife Abuse* (Beverly Hills: Sage).

Pennell, Joan (1987) "Ideology at a Canadian shelter for battered women: A reconstruction" *Women's Studies International Forum* 10, No. 2.

Pleck, Elizabeth (1987) *Domestic Tyranny: The Making of Social Policy against Family Violence from Colonial Times to the Present* (New York and Oxford: Oxford Univ. Press).

Police Monitoring and Research Group (1986) *Police Response to Domestic Violence* (LSPU).

Pooley, Leana (1986) "The Accident" *New Society* (3/1/86) (pp.5-6).

Postell, C. (1986) "Battered women: Understanding the problem" *Trial* 22.

Prime, Terenece and Walsh, Bernadette (1988) "Committals for breaches of matrimonial injunctions: A checklist and comment" *Family Law* 18 (pp.47-50).

Pugh, G. and Cohen N. (1984) "Presentation of marital problems in general practice" *The Practitioner* 228 (July 1984).

Radford, Jill (1987) "Policing male violence – policing women" in Hanmer and Maynard (ed.) (*op. cit.*).

Radford, Lorraine (1987) "Legalising woman abuse" in Hanmer and Maynard *op. cit.*

Radford, Lorraine (1988) *The Law and Domestic Violence Against Women* (Unpublished Ph.D. Thesis, Univ. of Bradford, Department of Applied Social Studies July 1988.

Rae, M. and Levin, J. (1983) "Ouster injunctions since Richards" *LAG Bulletin* December 1983 (pp.145-147)

Sanders, Andrew (1988) "Personal violence and public order: Prosecution of 'domestic' violence in England and Wales" *International Journal of Sociology of Law* Vol. 16, No. 3 (pp.359-382)

Saville, H. *et al.* (1981) "Sex roles, inequality and spouse abuse" *Australian and New Zealand Journal of Sociology* Vol. 17, No. 1 (pp.83-88)

Schechter, Susan (1982) *Women and Male Violence: The Visions and Struggles of the Battered Women's Movement* (London: Pluto Press)

Shupe, Anson, Stacey, William and Hazlewood, Lonnie (1987) *Violent Men, Violent Couples* (Lexington, Mass.: Lexington Books)

Smart, Carol. (1984) *The Ties that Bind: Law, Marriage, and Reproduction of Patriarchal Relations* (London: RKP)

Smart, Carol (1989) *Feminism and the Power of the Law* (London: Routledge)

Smith, Lorna (1989) *Domestic Violence: An Overview of the Literature* (Home Office Research and Planning Unit Report No. 107, H.M.S.O., London)

Stanko, Elizabeth (1985) *Intimate Intrusions: Women's Experience of Male Violence* (London: RKP)

Stanko, Elizabeth (1989) "Missing the mark? Policing battering" in Hanmer *et al.* (ed.) *(op. cit.)*

Stark, Evan and Flitcraft, Ann (n.d.) "Child Abuse and the battering of women: Are they related and how?" Paper presented at the National Family Violence Conference, Durham, New Hampshire.

Stark, Evan and Flitcraft, Ann (1983) "Social knowledge, social policy and the abuse of women: The case against patriarchal benevolence" in Finkelhor *et al.* (ed.) *(op.cit.)*

Stark, Fred and McEvoy, George (1970) "Middle class violence" *Psychology Today* Nov. 1970

Strube, Michael and Barbour, Linda S. (1983) "The decision to leave an abusive relationship: Economic dependence and psychological commitment" *Journal of Marriage and the Family* 45 (4) (pp.785-793)

Struder, Marlena (1984) "Wife-beating as a social problem: The process of definition" *International Journal of Women's Studies* 7 (5) (pp.412-422)

Taubman, S. (1986) "Beyond bravado: Sex roles and the exploitative male" *Social Work* 31 (Feb. 86) (pp.12-18)

Thompson, B.C. (1986) "Defending the battered wife: A challenge for defense attorneys" *Trial* 22 (pp.74-80)

Torgbor, Shan (1989) "Police intervention in domestic violence: A comparative review" *Family Law* Vol. 19, May 1989 (pp.195-198)

Trivedi, Parita (1984) "To deny our fullness: Asian women in the making of history" *Feminist Review* 17 (pp.37-50)

Turner, S. and Shapiro, C. "Battered women: Mourning the death of a relationship" *Social Work* 31 (Sept/Oct. 86) (p.372-6)

Walker, Lenore (1983) "The battered woman syndrome study" in Finkelhor *et al.* *(op.cit.)*

Walker, Lenore (1985) "Psychological impact of the criminalisation of domestic violence on victims" *Victimology* Vol. 10 (pp.281-300)

Wallis, J.H. (1973) "Matrimonial problems and the Citizens' Advice Bureaux: Reflections on a sample survey" *Marriage Guidance* Sept. 1983 (pp.334-337)

Wardell, Laurie, Gillespie, Dair and Leffler, Ann (1983) "Science and violence against wives" in Finkelhor *et al.* (ed.) *(op. cit.)*

Wasoff, Fran (1982) "Legal protection from wife beating: The processing of domestic assaults by Scottish protectors and criminal courts" *International Journal of the Sociology of Law* Vol. 10, No. 2 (pp.187-204)

Wexler, S. (1982) "Battered women and public policy" in Boneparth, E.(ed.) *Women, Power and Policy* (New York: Pergamon Press)

Williams, Catherine (1988) "Ouster orders, property adjustment and council housing" *Family Law* Vol. 18 (pp.438–443)

Williams, John (1985) "Marital rape" *Family Law* Vol. 15 (pp.99–101)

Wilson, Amrit (1984) *Finding a Voice: Asian Women in Britain* 3rd ed. (London: Virago)

Women's National Commission (1985) *Report to the Cabinet Office* (London: HMSO)

Wright, Moira (1980) "The Domestic Violence and Matrimonial Proceedings Act 1976: An evaluation" *New Law Journal* 130 (pp.127–129)

Yllo, Kersti (1983) "Using a feminist approach in quantitative research: A case study" in Finkelhor *et al* (ed.) (*op. cit.*)

Yllo, Kersti (1988) "Political and methodological debates in wife abuse research" in Yllo and Bograd (ed.) (*op. cit.*)

Yllo, Kersti and Bograd, Michele (1988) (ed.) *Feminist Perspectives on Wife Abuse* (Beverly Hills and London: Sage)

Zoomer, Olga J. (1989) "Policing woman battering in the Netherlands" in Hanmer, Radford, Stanko (ed.) *op. cit.*

GLOSSARY

ABH: actual bodily harm, resulting from assault.

ACCESS: term used with reference to the children of a relationship. If one parent has been granted custody (q.v.), the other parent is normally given regular times to see the children. "Staying access" involves overnight stays at the house of the non-custodial parent. If the non-custodial parent cannot be trusted not to abuse or abduct the children, the judge may specify "supervised access"; i.e. some other (named) adult has to be present throughout the visit.

AFFIDAVIT: a written sworn statement which is presented in court in support of an application for e.g. injunction or divorce. (Affidavits are not used in the magistrates' court).

ANCILLARY: additional legal applications which are attached to an "originating application". For example, in an originating application for divorce, division of property and custody. of the children are regarded as "ancillary" matters; and an injunction may be applied for "ancillary to" an application for divorce, or for damages or trespass.

CASE LAW: when a new law is introduced onto the statute books, it is interpreted in practice by judges in different courts, and there is a gradual process of clarification as particular points in the law are tested and taken to appeal in the higher courts; (High Court, Appeal Court, House of Lords.) Rulings made in the higher courts become binding on judges in the lower courts. These rulings are called "precedents" and constitute "case law".

CIVIL LAW: law concerned with disputes between individuals, rather than constituting a criminal offence. Civil law is aimed at such things as protection and righting wrongs rather than punishment. Civil cases are heard in the county court, the High Court, and the domestic magistrates' court.

COMMITTAL HEARING: in civil law, this is the hearing at which a man who is alleged to have broken a court order, thereby being in contempt of court (q.v.) will have his case heard. Committals are heard in open court, unlike the original injunction application. (The procedure in the magistrates' court is slightly different.)

CONTEMPT OF COURT: the offence of which a man is guilty if he breaks a court order by e.g. assaulting his partner. If found guilty of contempt of court, a man may be warned, fined, given a suspended sentence or sent to prison.

COURT ORDER: a general term which covers injunctions and other orders made in the county court (e.g. under the MHA, q.v.), and also personal and family protection orders made in the magistrates' court.

CRIMINAL LAW: involves prosecution for a criminal offence, e.g. an assault. Prosecution is usually undertaken on behalf of the state by the Crown Prosecution Service (q.v.) and the concern is punishment of the offender rather than protection of the victim. Criminal cases are heard in the magistrates' court and the Crown Court.

CROWN PROSECUTION SERVICE (CPS): the body which acts on behalf of the state, taking on cases on the recommendation of the police, and filtering out those in which they feel the prosecution case is not strong enough.

CUSTODY: often used as a general term in reference to the children of a relationship, but should technically be separated into custody (i.e. who has overall power to make decisions regarding a child's upbringing) and care and control (i.e. the day to day looking after of the child).

DVA, DVMPA: Domestic Violence and Matrimonial Proceedings Act, 1976, or simply the Domestic Violence Act. See Chapter 2.

DPMCA: Domestic Proceedings and Magistrates' Courts' Act, 1978. See Chapter 2.

DECREE NISI: an intermediate or "interlocutory" judgement in actions for divorce or annulment.

DECREE ABSOLUTE: the finalising of a divorce action.

EXCLUSION ORDER: an order that someone be excluded from a particular house or area surrounding it, and that s/he not return to it except as specified in the order. Strictly speaking, this term only applies when the individual has left the house and is prevented from returning. If s/he has to be removed from the house first, then the term ouster (q.v.) is used, as is also the case for all orders made under the MHA (q.v.).

EX PARTE: a case which is heard in emergency circumstances without the other party being present, or having notice served on him or her.

EXPEDITED: the term used instead of *ex parte* to refer to emergency applications for protection orders in the magistrates' courts.

FAMILY PROTECTION ORDER: an order obtained under DPMCA (q.v.) incorporating non-molestation and exclusion clauses.

GBH: grievous bodily harm, resulting from assault. This is a more serious injury than ABH (q.v.).

GREEN FORM SCHEME: a form of legal aid (q.v.) which can be granted by a solicitor immediately and covers a limited amount of legal advice, but does not cover going to court.

GUARDIAN AD LITEM: the term used to apply to the adult who represents a child or minor in a court case.

INJUNCTION: a court order which rules that a person named in the order should or should not do something. Breaking an injunction is "contempt of court" (q.v.). Normally someone who breaks an injunction has to be brought back to court for an appropriate penalty, such a fine or a warning, or (exceptionally) a prison sentence to be imposed. Although "injunction" is often used as a generic term to mean any kind of non-molestation or exclusion order, technically injunctions can only be issued in the county court or High Court, under the DVA or in proceedings for "tort" (q.v.)

INTER PARTES: literally "between the parties", i.e. a court hearing at which both contesting parties are present.

LEGAL AID: the system which can pay for legal expenses for certain actions for those on a low income. A married person with no income of her own can claim legal aid for taking action against her partner, even if their joint income is above the prescribed limit.

MHA: Matrimonial Homes Act, 1983. This Act can regulate occupation of the matrimonial home between married couples, and lays down the criteria under which ousters (q.v.) can now be obtained.

OUSTER: a court order which orders that someone should leave the shared or matrimonial home, and not return to it for a specified period.

PERSONAL PROTECTION ORDER: a court order, obtained in the magistrates' court under the DPMCA (q.v.), ordering that a married person not assault or molest his wife and/or children. The equivalent of a non-molestation order obtained in the county court.

PETITIONER: the person initiating an application for e.g. divorce. In other cases, the term "applicant" is more properly used.

POWERS OF ARREST: may be attached to certain injunctions and protection orders, namely those made under DVA, DPMCA, and ancillary to divorce, but not to undertakings, or to orders made under the MHA or in civil "tort" proceedings. If a power of arrest is attached to an order, the police may exercise their discretion and arrest a man if they have reasonable grounds for believing he has broken the order, even if he has not otherwise committed an arrestable offence, and he must be held in custody and brought before the court within twenty four hours.

RESPONDENT: the person against whom an application is made.

RETURN DATE: date by which a case (which may have been heard *ex parte* or expedited) returns to court for a further full hearing.

SERVICE OF NOTICE: when notice of a court hearing is served on the respondent. This is necessary for all court hearings except in emergency circumstances, when it may be heard *ex parte*. There are set periods of notice according to the legislation used, but this may be abridged in certain circumstances if allowed by the court.

STATUTORY POWERS: powers given to the court under a

particular law or statute.

SUBSTITUTED SERVICE: when notice of a court hearing is served on someone other than the respondent, because after repeated attempts the respondent cannot be found. Substituted service has to be agreed by the court.

TORT: an action or omission which causes injury and which creates a claim for damages in the injured person. Injunctions may be applied for ancillary (q.v.) to a tort action.

UNDERTAKINGS: a promise made in county court or High Court which technically has the status of a court order. Often a man will offer an undertaking rather than accept an injunction, and the woman may accept in order to avoid a contested hearing. The magistrates' courts are not empowered to accept undertakings of this kind. See our discussion in Chapters 2, 4 and 7.